Smoke Over Birkenau

SMOKE OVER BIRKENAU

❊

LIANA MILLU

Translated from the Italian by Lynne Sharon Schwartz

NORTHWESTERN UNIVERSITY PRESS
Evanston, Illinois

Northwestern University Press
www.nupress.northwestern.edu

Originally published 1986 in Italian under the title *Il fumo di Birkenau*. Copyright © 1986 by Editrice La Giuntina, Firenze. English translation published 1991 by The Jewish Publication Society, Philadelphia. Northwestern University Press edition published 1997 by arrangement with The Jewish Publication Society. All rights reserved.

Printed in the United States of America

10   9   8   7   6   5

ISBN 978-0-8101-1569-9

Contents

Foreword

Liana Millu's *Smoke Over Birkenau* is one of the most powerful European testimonies to come from the women's lager at Auschwitz-Birkenau and by far the most affecting among Italian accounts. It consists of six narratives, all revolving around the specifically feminine aspects of the prisoners' wretched and minimal lives. For a variety of reasons, the women's situation was a good deal worse than that of the men: first, less physical endurance, coupled with work more arduous and degrading than the labors imposed on the men; the agonies of disrupted families; and above all the haunting presence of the crematoria, located right in the middle of the women's camp, inescapable, undeniable, their ungodly smoke rising from the chimneys to contaminate every day and every night, every moment of respite or illusion, every dream and timorous hope.

The author rarely appears in the foreground; she is rather a penetrating eye, a superbly vigilant consciousness recording and transcribing, in uniformly dignified and measured tones, events that were themselves beyond human measure. Each narrative closes with a muted, funereal knell: a life has been snuffed out, and it is remarkable how weighty these individual, private deaths become, each tragic in its distinct way, and how deeply they are incised on our spirits, in contrast to the millions of anonymous, statistical deaths.

Each of these human dilemmas in an inhuman world is suffused with an aura of pure lyrical sorrow, never distorted by anger or unseemly self-pity, and of painful worldly wisdom — proof that the author did not suffer in vain.

Primo Levi

Translator's Note

The women referred to throughout the text as *blockowas*, *stubowas*, and Kapos of work squads and barracks are themselves prisoners granted positions of authority at the lower levels of the lager hierarchy but still subject to the same perils as ordinary prisoners. On the other hand, the guards and soldiers referred to are part of the SS, an army that was distinct from the *Wehrmacht*, or regular German army, and that, among other things, controlled the camps.

L. S. S.

Lili Marlene

There was a bit of confusion that morning because of the medical check the night before. A number of women had been sent to be disinfected for scabies, leaving the Kommandos all disorganized, and in their zeal to make up for the missing "merchandise," the Kapos were quarreling over the ones remaining, like market vendors disputing some select basket of dainties. It was the crack of dawn and I was shivering with cold, yet I couldn't help grinning as I watched the rival Kapos in their violent tugs of war over the unlucky victims.

I greeted Jeannette with the major concern of the day: "Do you think it'll rain?"

Jeannette peered out to the east, streaked by pale gray light, then to the night sky in the west, studded with stars, and concluded that it wouldn't rain. This was cheering news, to say the least, and I was just turning around to reply when all at once I was seized by the arm and dragged to one side.

I could guess what this meant. "But I'm already in a Kommando," I cried. "I'm assigned to a Kommando, *Frau Kapo.*"

Jeannette was calling my name reproachfully, which only made things worse. She was probably thinking the usual: I was good for nothing, I never fought back. How could I let myself be abducted so easily?

The strong little Kapo who had kidnapped me shunted me into line with the notoriously awful Kommando 110: it worked on road construction and was made up almost entirely of Hungarians. I looked around fearfully. My new companions must have come to the camp before I did, since their hair was already grown back—it stuck out from under their kerchiefs. They regarded me with blank, impersonal stares, showing not the slightest interest, except for the woman on my right, who asked rather half-heartedly where I was from.

"Italian," I said. "You?"

"Hungarian," was the grudging reply, and she promptly turned away, as if there were no earthly reason to waste another glance or word on me.

I had worked with Hungarians before—tough, resilient women who had no patience with anyone who complained about the drudgery. The singular response the endless ups and downs of our wretched life could elicit from them was *"Micinaio, micinaio?"* "What can I do, what can I do?" and they would repeat it over and over like a broken record till my nerves were shot.

In my circumstances, no doubt, a Hungarian would have said, *"Micinaio, micinaio?"* Actually, I must have said it to myself, because I reacted unconsciously, on the spur of the moment. When the Kapo passed, I found myself stepping out of line, ready to accost her.

"Bitte, Frau Kapo, I . . ."

She knew perfectly well what was on my mind, though, and didn't even give me a chance to open my mouth, simply wheeled around, smacked me in the face, and said, "Get back in line," making it quite clear there was nothing I could do.

"Get back in line!" she repeated, raising her fist. It was

somewhat lighter now, so I could get a better look at her. She had a puny little face, neither beautiful nor very young, with thin lips, a narrow nose, and sharp black eyes glinting spitefully under a furrowed brow. There was a certain brittleness to her lean, restless figure—a type who in civilian life would be labeled high-strung. The smack stung my cheek, and I surreptitiously gave her a dirty look. Starting the day being hit was a bad omen. God only knew how it would end up.

Even more painful was being separated from the French girls, who were my good friends. In this foreign Kommando, I was definitely unwanted and felt like a stray dog. Tears sprang to my eyes. I struggled to keep them back since crying was considered a contemptible sign of weakness, but they ran down my face and into my mouth, tasting of salt.

"Don't cry." It was a gentle voice not far off. I turned in astonishment: two rows away stood a very young, pretty girl with a friendly smile. It wasn't worth crying about, she said. The Kapo was so horrid, she went on in broken German, that if I paid any attention to her I'd be crying all day long. I was startled at her refinement—she was evidently a well-brought-up young lady—not to mention her gracious attitude, which as far as I knew was unheard of in the lager. Above all, I was puzzled by the vague sense of having seen that face somewhere before. Surely we must have met, but I couldn't place her.

The girl must have felt the same, for she too looked at me as if straining to piece together fragments of distant memory. Then it all came back in a flash.

"You're Lili Marlene!" I cried. I was immensely relieved: the Hungarian girl had been a good friend to me in the early days, working in lager A. We had given her that nickname because she loved the plaintive song that sounded like humanity's melancholy sigh in the face of devastating forces.

"And you're Lianka!" Lili was as pleased as I was.

Jostling our way through the rows of icy faces watching in scornful surprise, we managed to embrace. Lili's comforting reality worked like a charm to dispel my bad mood and any evil omens. I wouldn't be alone and friendless in a hostile Kommando; she would protect me against the abuse and bullying that newcomers were inevitably subjected to.

She turned to a tall redheaded girl. "Change places with Lianka," she asked. Without a word, the redhead took my place and I was next to Lili.

I was amazed, up close, to see how well groomed she was, how neat her clothes looked. Her dress wasn't shabby and raggedy—quite the contrary. She even boasted a little pastel-blue apron to match the kerchief covering her beautiful jet-black curls, which had grown in and framed her pale, delicate face. Her metal bowl didn't hang from her hip the way mine did, on an improvised loop made of straw pulled from my mat, but was concealed in one of those pouches patched together from strips of blanket, which, in the inspired hands of many of the lager's proletariat, could become an elegant sample of craftsmanship.

"Why, you look lovely," I said warmly. "What pretty things you have." Lili smiled with pleasure and instinctively smoothed down her hair.

"The Kapo sometimes gives me her sewing to do," she explained, "so I can 'organize' a bit of thread and mend my clothes."

Never in a million years would I spend my Sunday afternoons sewing, I asserted. I didn't care how ragged I got. Sundays were for sleeping. Anyway, why should I give a damn what I looked like? I didn't have any *kochany* in the lager, I certainly didn't have to fix myself up for anyone.

"It's for our own sake," Lili scolded. She would have lectured me further, but as soon as the words were out, a tall, gaunt, disagreeable woman who had been gaping nosily at us glanced sardonically at a wan woman beside her, obviously her sister. Then she turned back to us and remarked cattily: "But Lili has a *kochany*. Sure she does. He's terrific, really high class. Lili's *kochany* is Grade A, prime."

The young girl turned beet red. "You're so mean, Elenka," she cried. "How can you say such things? What did I ever do? You're just a liar!" Her face betrayed her, though. She looked like someone whose most precious secret is dragged out and made into a laughing-stock.

The scrawny Elenka was about to retort, but the Kommandos started down the *Lagerstrasse* and we weren't allowed to speak. As we slowly approached the gate, the band stationed at the command post broke into a sprightly marching tempo, and after a last-minute check of shoes and collars, the Kapos advanced at the head of their Kommandos like officers leading their battalions. The lager's "red bands," all smartly arrayed, gave us the once-over before handing us over to be inspected by the German officers. Since this was the most significant as well as exacting task of their entire day, nothing escaped their scrutiny—not one smudged bowl or imperfectly polished clog.

"Heads up, hands still, chests out!" they shouted incessantly, as with each command our posture stiffened, becoming more martial.

I was pleased to discover that since Kommando 110 was so small we wouldn't be escorted by *Posten* (SS guards) furnished with police dogs. Once past the gate we turned left along an unfamiliar road. My former Kommando used to head straight on down the road leading to Auschwitz, but today's route, going by the station and the men's lager, offered a dazzling array of novelty; indeed I was so taken with the panorama that for the moment I even neglected Lili.

There was nothing much to see on the left except a broad expanse of damp, drab fields. Veiled in mist, broken only by thick, gloomy clumps of trees, they seemed to be waking dolefully to face the day. But on our right loomed the formidable railroad station: there was the arch my train had passed under, there the very spot where I had gotten off. An avalanche of memories assaulted me. So many of those who got off with me were gone. Perhaps they had merely preceded me, and one day I too would follow down the same dark path.

Groups of high-spirited young soldiers from the guard corps ambled about, laughing and joking, smoking their pipes. With hands in their pockets and submachine guns slung over their shoulders, they watched us go by, their fresh boyish faces pleasantly ruddy in the biting morning air. Behind them we could glimpse others sitting in the office, where the lamps were still lit.

"Look at those chairs!" I said to Lili, who gave a nod rich with nostalgia.

Any "civilians" hearing me marvel or seeing the wonder and longing in Lili's gesture would no doubt have thought us out of our minds. But we were old lager inmates who for months now had sat on nothing but the hard ground, and so for us those humble furnishings were a veritable poem of yearning and nostalgia. Where there are chairs there's a house, and a table, maybe even a white tablecloth. Oh that beloved lost world! Would we ever find our way back?

After a short stretch we reached the electrified barbed wire fence of the men's *Quarantänelager* (Quarantine lager), interspersed with tall wooden towers from whose windows the guards surveyed us with bored faces.

"Is it a long way to go?" I asked Lili.

"No," she said, "we're almost there."

Soon the Kommando turned off onto a path with a narrow-gauge track running along it, which led to a large open space circled by trees. At the far end stood a wooden shack, and beside it a half-ruined little chapel, bereft of crosses and sacred images. Only a few faded stars painted on a piece of blue plaster recalled that once upon a time those walls must have displayed scenes of the heavenly hosts.

These days the chapel was used to store the Kommando's shovels, hoes, and other tools, and the women were rushing over to grab the lightest ones.

"Here we are," said Lili.

Again I was in a state of dread. I didn't know how to do the work, the Kapo would surely beat me, and who could come to my aid?

"Let me stay with you," I begged Lili abjectly, like a stray dog.

Of course I could, she said, and I mustn't be afraid. With that, she made a dash for the chapel and I followed at her heels, but since the best tools had been taken, we had to settle for two huge, heavy spades.

"It's as tall as I am." Lili grinned, holding it up against

her shoulder. I was struck once more by the gentle charm of her face, especially her eyes—dark as chocolate, large, and sparkling with life.

"Come to my *lora*," she said, breaking into a run and leaping over puddles of mud. "Come on, hurry up, before the Kapo gets here."

I didn't know what a *"lora"* was, but I was content to tag along after the amiable Lili, racing across the clearing to where the tracks ended. There we found five enormous tram cars lined up, the sort used for hauling freight, surrounded by heaps of sand. Farther off, the clearing dipped down into a hollow, where part of the Kommando was already digging in the sand, which they would relay up to us by way of a long chain of shovels.

"Come over here," said Lili. I followed her to the third *lora*—I realized that was what they called the tram cars— and began tossing in sand that the silent redheaded girl was piling up beside me. Five women worked at each tram, and unfortunately, our group included the two sisters who had spoken so sarcastically to Lili this morning. In fact, with every shovelful of sand Elenka tossed on the pile, she managed to make a good bit land on my feet. She did it with an air of challenge, too, in case I should dare to protest, which of course I wasn't about to do. I didn't even attempt to avoid it. As a recent arrival, and an Italian at that, I knew this sort of churlishness was to be expected, so I resolved to maintain my dignity and ignore it. I would simply work hard and try to warm up.

The Kapo, meanwhile, was striding up and down watching us and badgering. "Fill up those trams! Fill them up to the top!" she yelled relentlessly, and only when they were loaded with huge mounds of sand was she satisfied. She ordered us to get moving, and under her vigilant eye, we bent our backs beneath the iron fittings of the cars and laboriously slid them onto the tracks. At long last the Kapo—Mia was her name—turned and went into the shack.

"She's going to light the fire," said redheaded Aërgi wistfully, without a hint of envy or rancor.

"She wants to have the place all warmed up for him," Elenka snapped in her vinegary tone, and her sister observed that we had at least two trips to go before "he" arrived.

Baffled, I asked Lili what they were talking about. She explained tersely that the Kapo had a *kochany* who visited every day when he passed by with his Kommando. That was why Mia was lighting the stove. They would cook and generally amuse themselves in the shack. He was German too and could get anything he needed.

"What does he look like?" I asked curiously.

Lili made some gesture that vaguely signified "handsome." She seemed uncomfortable, just as in the morning.

"And what about your *kochany*?" I teased, harking back to Elenka's nasty crack. "Will you point him out to me?"

"I don't have any *kochany!*" Lili blushed and was flustered. I realized that, given her innocence and modesty, she would never confide her secret: it was the one thing she could call her own and nurture tenderly in the privacy of her heart—a tiny flame carefully shielded from the savagery of the insidious shadows all around. I dropped the subject. Silently, I helped haul the tram onto the wet tracks and guided it back along the path we had taken before. Up at the main road, a small group unloaded the sand and piled it into a kind of trench, while we paused to take a break, leaning against the cars.

The early morning mist had vanished and the pale sun

cast weak rays, but no warmth, on the countryside. And yet despite the pallor of the light, everything suddenly looked different: the fields stood out luminously, tinged with the last green of autumn and the bright red bricks of a half-built house. It definitely wouldn't rain today, and this, in our misery, was the greatest of all possible blessings.

As the moments crept by, we glanced warily over toward the trees every so often, watching for Mia's dread shape. Sure enough, in a little while we spied her in the distance, waving her club and glaring until we got the trams sliding swiftly on the tracks. Then it was back down into the quarry again to refill them—the same operation, once, twice, three times, with Mia coming out of the shack periodically to curse and threaten us: the cars weren't full enough, the trips not fast enough. Elenka and her sister bickered, Aërgi and Lili were silent, so my only distraction was looking around. A bluish wisp of smoke fluttered merrily from the chimney of the shack. The Kapo must have a good fire going. I pictured the leaping flames and crackling wood, the glowing red sparks flying up the chimney, and imagined how it would feel to sit there with the gentle heat seeping through my pores, warming me through and through. As I gripped the icy wet iron of the tram, I strove to conjure up the sensation of heat, to warm my cold stiff hands by the power of suggestion.

I was in a trance, lost in fantasies of glowing stoves and fireplaces that warmed me in memory, when a violent shove sent my head slamming against the iron bar. It was Mia, hurtling down the narrow path toward the main road, dealing out smacks and shoves as she passed the women bent over the cars.

"She's having a fit because he's not here yet," commented

Aërgi, who had also been pushed roughly. This must have been the case—the women at the tram ahead were saying the same thing. Every eye was fixed on Mia's slender shape headed for the road, where she waited with evident anxiety, pacing back and forth, then pausing to peer in the direction of the *Quarantänelager*. As my tram drew near, I was terrified. I was the closest to her, and her face was screwed up with frustration and impatience. She would hit me when I passed, I just knew it, and the agony of anticipation was far worse than any real and unforeseen blow.

I turned to Lili. "She's going to hit me right now," I said. But she only gave an absent-minded nod of commiseration. She too gazed straight ahead down the road, past where the Kapo stood, as if awaiting some thrilling apparition.

I was staring like the rest when suddenly, in a tone of vast relief, Elenka burst out, "There he is!"

"There he is!" The women's faces relaxed and brightened, as if a crushing burden had been lifted.

The course of our Kapo's romance was followed with extreme and universal interest, the women being well aware that if Mia's *kochany* was late or failed to show up, she would storm about, taking out her resentment and vexation on them, whereas so long as the honeymoon in the shack lasted, they would reap the priceless benefit of a few hours of peace. Small wonder that the entire Kommando was ardently absorbed in the vicissitudes of the love affair, wishing the Kapos joy from the bottom of their hearts—for in the nature of things, a man and woman in love tend to become, however unwillingly, rather more generous and well disposed. Thus Elenka's cry virtually throbbed with the joy of deliverance. And watching the Kapo make her way down the road, her face softened and eased in a way I wouldn't have dreamed possible, I too felt liberated from the nightmare of the expected beating and gave thanks for the heaven-sent *kochany*.

We had reached the road now too and spied an unwieldy tank cart, the kind used for draining sewers, lumbering toward us, dragged by a bunch of prisoners in the role of horses. As it lurched along, giving off a nauseating smell of sewage, the young guard in the driver's seat whistled a tune and marked the rhythm with his riding crop. A little ways back, their Kapo, tall, powerfully built, and quite elegant in a sporty overcoat, sauntered along with his hands in his pockets. His gray and purple striped lager beret was tilted jauntily to one side, giving his face—handsome in a vulgar sort of way—a radiantly self-assured air of well-being.

When he got closer, he signaled for the cart to keep moving. "Righto," cried the guard merrily, in a tone laced with sly, tacit allusion, and the Kapo turned off down the path toward Mia.

She was ready for him, her eyes beaming a welcome. After exchanging a few words, they started for the clearing, and this time she was in such haste that her passage was peaceful—all we had to do was keep solicitously out of the way.

A trace of perfume rippled in their wake even after the door of the shack closed. Once they were safely inside, the whole Kommando promptly put down their tools, abandoned the trams, and stretched their weary arms. On every side the women were saying, "We'll be okay for a while now." Love must truly be a gift of the gods, I mused, if it could grant these brief spells of respite to miserable human "merchandise" like us.

We passed the time of day, now and then making a trip

down to the quarry and filling the cars, though the intervals between trips grew longer and longer. People were laughing and fooling around, and I suddenly felt like hearing Lili sing her favorite song.

"Sing me 'Lili Marlene,'" I urged, and wouldn't leave her alone until she began, very softly:

> *Bei der Kaserne, vor dem grossen Tor*
> *stand eine Laterne, und steht sie noch davor . . .*

"Underneath the lantern, by the barrack gate . . ." As I listened to Lili's subdued voice, the plaintive melody reverberated in my heart. Vivid images from my former life sprang up and hovered before me, carrying me far away from the trams and the sand, from everything in Birkenau. I was barely following the words, yet the song brought such delight that I asked Lili to sing it one more time, and again I coaxed her until she gave in.

Back at the road, Lili and I sat down on the ledge of a tram while the others unloaded the sand. She didn't want to sing any more. Instead she pulled a tiny fragment of mirror from her pocket and examined her face, biting her lips to redden them and arranging the curls that escaped from the blue kerchief.

"Your hair's really grown in nicely," I noted. She enjoyed hearing that, I could tell, so I added that I bet she used to fuss over her looks, back home.

"Oh, I really did." She told me her family had owned a perfume shop on a main avenue of Budapest, quite a splendid shop with sparkling windows and the finest perfumes. She was mad for perfume. She used it all the time, even though her mother scolded.

"Did you use as much as the Kapo's *kochany?*" I teased,

but immediately saw that this kind of remark was unwelcome.

Lili began speaking of her old life in Budapest, a distant, serene, gracious life that had vanished in a flash, crumbled to dust, and all because of a man-made law. Everything so painstakingly built up was shattered in minutes—houses were deserted, families scattered as they fled, the whole world was transformed overnight into a treacherous jungle.

"But it'll all be over soon," she said confidently, studying her young face in the broken mirror.

"Do you really think so?" I asked, for the simple pleasure of hearing her say yes.

And she did say it: of course it would be over soon, by Christmas we'd all be back home. In her calm tone there wasn't the shadow of a doubt that her house would still be standing.

I couldn't help wondering how old she was. Just turned seventeen, she told me. As she cleaned her fingernails with a stick she found on the ground, she kept glancing over at the shack.

"Do you sew for the Kapo every day?"

"Not every day. Actually, I haven't done any for a while."

No sooner had she said this than the door opened and the Kapo appeared, her face flushed and animated.

"The seamstress! Where's my seamstress?" she cried, waving a beautiful, soft white sweater.

Lili went over, and the Kapo pointed out the sleeves. When she noticed us watching, she dashed forward, shaking her fist.

"What's the idea? What do you think you're doing, you goddamn bitches? What's going on here?"

So we bent back over our shovels, and as Mia stood glaring at us, hands on her hips, the sand rapidly heaped up and flew into the trams. Lili walked to the chapel and sat down on the crumbling old bricks in the doorway. The thread and scissors the Kapo had given her lay in her lap while she gazed lovingly at the white sweater. How wonderful it must be to touch that rich, clean, warm fabric; I remembered how it once felt to bury my face in a bunch of flowers or a patch of velvet—but had I really ever felt such things?

With just the four of us, it was much more difficult to push the tram. We couldn't keep up with the others, indeed we could barely move it; the women at the next tram, terrified of what the Kapo might do when she returned, screamed vile insults to urge us on.

It might go more easily, I thought, with some distraction to pass the time. So though I was straining with all my might, I tried to strike up a conversation with Aërgi, the redheaded girl beside me. Where she was from, what did she use to do back home, was she all alone in the lager? In short, the usual overtures one made in the camp, with anyone new who appeared halfway decent.

Aërgi was from Budapest, she said, where she had been a music student.

"Oh, you're from Budapest too? Did you know Lili there?" A foolish question, I realized the moment I asked. Budapest was hardly the village square that everyone crossed ten times a day. But to my great surprise Aërgi said yes, she had known Lili before. They often met at concerts and music clubs. I was curious about the Lili of back then, a Lili I would never know.

"What was she like? Pretty?"

Very pretty, Aërgi said, and always dressed in bright colors: she liked being noticed and admired. She was an only child and her parents indulged her like a baby.

"Well, she's in luck now," I remarked, looking over at Lili on the chapel steps. "That's certainly not too strenuous. I wouldn't mind working for the Kapo myself."

Aërgi shook her head. "No. No good work for Mia," she said in her broken German. "Better stay away."

When I disagreed—it struck me as infinitely preferable to push a needle and "organize" thread than drag around a shovel—Aërgi became more explicit.

"Mia *kochany* make joke with Lili. The Kapo very jealous. She see this, Lili right to crematorium."

"Oh, that sounds like a bit much," I protested. But Aërgi was convinced. All the fellow had to do was give Lili a nod or smile in passing, and young and pretty as she was, she forgot she was nothing but an *Arbeitstück*, a "work unit." She imagined she might still be regarded as a human being. Look how she blushed whenever she saw him. Not that she did anything wrong, poor Lili, just turned red and let her eyes trail after him with yearning. Still, the minute Mia noticed, there would be hell to pay.

"Do you think Lili's really in love with him?" I asked Aërgi. The mere notion stirred me with pity. If it was true, then my young friend was burdened not only by the lager itself, but by the searing vulnerability of passion as well.

"Poor Lili," I sighed, and sensible Aërgi nodded in sympathy.

All afternoon Lili sat quietly sewing on the chapel steps. On one of our trips down to the clearing we found her waiting for us all excited, looking almost happy. She held out some cabbage leaves and insisted that Aërgi and I share her precious gift. We fell on it greedily. This was an incredible treat, especially as our palates were practically deadened by overcooked turnips. We couldn't stop marveling at the forgotten taste of fresh raw greens.

I noticed that Lili kept two leaves wrapped up in her apron. Was she saving them for supper, I teased, or planning to have them stolen by some Ukrainian?

"I'm going to see Madame Louise tonight, to have her read my cards," she said. "If I bring her two cabbage leaves, it'll save me a slice of bread."

I found this immensely intriguing, for I have always held palm-readers and fortune tellers in quasi-religious awe. Moreover, I had heard talk of this Madame Louise, a Tunisian woman whose gift was reputedly prodigious.

"Oh, I'd like to do it too! How much does she charge?"

Usually three slices of bread, said Lili, slightly less than half a ration. But for the shortened version, two would be enough. "Why don't you come along?"

Despite all my rational objections, I was dying to go, and so this invitation was the perfect excuse.

We agreed that after the evening roll-call and bread distribution, Lili would pick me up and we'd go to Barrack 15, where Madame Louise slept. Our plan kept us in a state of eager anticipation for the rest of the day, and the time passed fairly quickly and calmly. Every now and then the Kapo opened her door to shout and threaten, and even dropped by several times to give a few random smacks, but once these official duties were fulfilled, she went back inside. The pale blue wisp of smoke still fluttered up from the chimney, and whenever Mia opened the door, the keen smell of frying pancakes wafted over to us—a blend of burning grease and sugar that sent shivers up and down our spines like a wildly voluptuous caress, making even our teeth tingle. Behind those four pathetic wooden walls was a genuine garden of earthly delights!

Finally the distant gong of the men's *Quarantänelager* sounded its first stroke, alerting the Kommandos to head back. The tank cart came punctually up the road, the young guard climbed down to knock on the door of the shack, and the two Kapos came right out. He looked heartily contented, as would any man who had spent a good day beside a warm fire, with plenty of food, and a woman near at hand. Pulling on his gloves, he signaled for the men dragging the cart to move along.

"Quick, quick! You look like you're fast asleep," he called out, squeezing Mia's hand. As the cart set off, he took a shortcut around a bend to catch up with it on the main road. We had paused for a moment at a tricky point on the tracks and saw him turn to Lili as he passed.

"Hey, little one. Did you do a good job on my sweater?"

He didn't stop or even slow down, merely smiled. Lili's eyes drank in his smile and she blushed, as usual.

The next minute he was up at the road where the cart waited. The second gong sounded, the Kommandos headed back, and he pressed his men to hurry; their bony backs bent lower over the bars as the cart staggered toward their lager.

The day was over at last. We left our trams, retracing the path we had taken in the morning. Once again, music greeted us at the gate and the officers counted us, but this time the review by the "red bands" was less meticulous, for we had to hurry to the barracks and line up for the evening roll-call. The auxiliaries were already circulating; any minute, the whistles would blow and the martial *Achtung* of the first inspections would ring out.

Since our barrack was at the far end of the camp, right beside a crematorium, the auxiliary always got to us last. The guards took advantage of the extra time to give out the bread while we waited, which had its good and bad points: good because we were spared waiting on another line after roll-call, and bad because it was torture to get through the hour or hours of inspection with my bread under my arm. Each evening became an endurance test as I wrestled with the most ferocious temptation. I would start out full of resolve, hiding the bread inside my dress for a quarter of an hour or so, then take it out to gaze lovingly and sniff with passion, until the struggle between desire and the wisdom of deferred gratification culminated in my ripping into the bread like a starving beast, destroying in no time what was the object of endless inner conflict.

That evening the struggle was compounded by our plan to visit Madame Louise. Time and again I sequestered the bread in the safe harbor of my dress, determined not to remove it until after roll-call. But as always, my efforts proved futile. I had planned to save enough to pay decently for the smallest possible fortune, but in the end, the paltry bit remaining seemed almost an insult to the fortune teller, and so with a desperate, bitter insouciance I sent it the way of the rest and watched my fortune vanish.

Roll-call that evening seemed endless anyway. The auxiliary took forever to arrive, and it was nearly two hours before the whistle released us. The instant we broke ranks came the daily stampede to squeeze into the barrack. Hundreds of women thronged around the tiny door, pushing and mauling each other to get a few extra moments of rest. I stood aside as always, waiting patiently.

"I'll be by for you in a little while," Lili called. "Do you want to come and wash?"

That invitation I declined. My hands were dirty, but I hadn't the strength to face another battle to get into the washroom. In any case, the water always stopped running just when there was the greatest demand. I told Lili I'd wash in the morning with the so-called tea. I'd been pushed around enough for one day.

Lili went off alone to wash and fix herself up, while I went into the barrack and lay down on the straw mat, where the others had already spread their blankets. And of course it never failed: when I saw the women who had resisted the pangs of hunger during roll-call relishing their bread, nibbling one morsel after another with sensuous stinginess, I was overcome by a totally irrational and rankling envy. The nerve of it! They were eating and I had nothing left. Though it was my own doing, I watched them grudgingly, unable to shake my sense of injustice.

It was dark by the time Lili came rushing in to find me. She still had almost half a ration of bread wrapped in her apron. "Ready?" she asked excitedly. I got myself up and we set off for Block 15.

The road between the barracks was a morass of puddles and thick slime—with every other step our heavy clogs got stuck. The mud was so deep that we needed both hands to help each other tug them out, meanwhile taking care not to tumble in headfirst.

"It's just like in your song." I laughed and Lili began

singing. When she got to the line, "And I smile and think of you," I gave her a friendly hug and said, "Who are you thinking of? Your *kochany?* Are you really in love?"

Lili broke away. She wasn't in love at all, she declared — I must be crazy. But her marvelous eyes, all aglow, proved that even in a *Vernichtungslager*, an extermination camp, a thought and a smile could transform number A5480 into a breathless, at times even happy, young girl.

And so we slogged through the muddy quicksand, kidding around and falling all over each other, our path lit by giant bursts of flame from the nearest crematorium, until at last we reached Barrack 15. Lili walked down the narrow aisle between the rows of bunks asking everyone, "Where is Madame Louise?" We were at one of the last nooks when a somber voice said, "I am Madame Louise."

We paused, straining our eyes to see into the shadows. At first it was all a blur, but as my eyes adjusted to the dark I made out the motionless form of a woman crouched against the back wall. On her knees lay what looked like a little mound of paper. She stared mutely with enigmatic Asian eyes, as very slowly she chewed on a piece of bread.

"Could you read the cards for me?" whispered Lili. She unwrapped the bread and two cabbage leaves from her apron to show she was prepared to pay what was necessary.

"Ah, so you want your cards read?" echoed Madame Louise, leaning toward us and shuffling the pieces of cardboard on her knees. The cards were drawn by hand with lettering that looked Arabic, which naturally heightened our sense of awe.

"Pick one with your left hand and think of what you care about most," she said in her somber voice.

Lili followed her instructions. We bent over the mat, where Madame Louise ritualistically laid out the cards as if on an altar rail, to conjure up the mighty and unfathomable powers governing our woeful lives.

"A *la cabeza, al corazón, al hígado, a lo que no esperas,*" she muttered, arranging them in the form of a cross.

"A *la cabeza* . . ." At the head, Lili had the ace of hearts, a great love. Someone was thinking of her. But then came two spades, which meant she had to be careful lest he bring her sorrow.

At the *corazón* was a good woman who loved her and grieved for her. Oh, how she grieved!

"My mother," said Lili, peering more intently at the cards.

She had to be on her guard, though, because there was another woman close by, a wicked, powerful woman—none other than the bad luck Queen of Spades—who was jealous and would try to harm her. Also, a change was on the way, a great change. . . .

"Could it be a trip?" asked Lili. My heart was pounding as I waited for the answer. A trip could only mean the end of the war and our return home.

"Yes, it is a trip," Madame Louise confirmed, "a very long trip, so long that I can't even see where it ends. . . ."

Lili turned to me. "It could take me a week to get home from here."

"A week on those cattle cars, sure. But they'd never send us back the way we came. We'll go home on the Red Cross train, on the sleepers." I couldn't picture our illustrious homecoming any other way—if we ever did get home, that is.

"This trip will be very soon. The pentagram here means
. . ."

But we never did get to find out what the pentagram
meant. The *Lagerkapo*'s shrill whistle blared through the
camp and at once the guards yelled for *Lagerruhe*, silence
from now on. Whoever didn't belong here had to get out.
Our barrack was unfortunately a ways off, and there was that
damned mud to traipse through. Lili quickly handed
Madame Louise the cabbage leaves and asked her to cut
herself two slices of bread. Just for spite, though, a fat guard
armed with a whip pounced on us. *Lagerruhe*, she yelled,
and violently shoved us out.

"My bread! I have to get my bread back!" Lili shrieked
wildly. The guard couldn't care less: she lashed out and
grazed us with the scorching whip, so we had no choice but
to forget the bread and make a run for it.

"Maybe Madame Louise will save you the leftover piece,"
I consoled Lili on the way back, as we performed fantastic
balancing acts, trying not to lose our clogs in the deep mud.
Finally we got to our barrack, which was totally silent.

"*Schnella, schnella* (quick, quick)," the guard at the door
grumbled in the peculiar Slavicized German that was the
lager's lingua franca. "*Lagerruhe! Schlafen, schnella!*"

I said good night to Lili and went to my mat, where the
others were already sleeping. Luckily my place was at the
edge, so I could slip under the covers without disturbing
anyone. Only Jeannette, who was used to snuggling up close
to me, shifted around when she felt me shiver against her
warm back.

"So what did she say?" she mumbled sleepily, for I had
told her about our expedition.

"There's going to be a great change soon. A trip," I reported, omitting the fact that this referred specifically to Lili.

"A trip? When is the war ending?" cried Jeannette, sitting up on the mat, suddenly wide awake. And being an impulsive, enthusiastic type, she leaned over to wake Stella, who slept all curled up at our feet.

"Stella! Stella! Madame Louise said the war's almost over!"

"Yes, it's almost over," I affirmed, by now utterly convinced that this was the salient outcome of our visit. "Madame Louise told the little Hungarian girl from my Kommando."

Stella sat up too, and I was preparing to give a thorough account of all I thought I remembered, except that angry voices, in various languages, were calling for silence.

"*Ruhe! Cihò! Taisez-vous!*"

So Stella, Jeannette, and I hugged each other for joy and fell asleep buoyed by hope and faith, our hearts at ease.

I don't know if this is a general tendency or peculiar to people of volatile temperament, but I went to sleep smiling, in a calm, contented mood, only to wake the next morning feeling quite the contrary. The weather, too, had taken a turn for the worse: the road was draped in fog and the mud seemed to have thickened and spread overnight, leaving the barracks bogged down in slime. Women who had been outside sliding around in it grumbled as they scraped it off their hands and clothes.

"It's going to rain," said Lili, standing beside me.

"You can say that again." I seemed to take a perverse pleasure in wallowing in our misery. "It'll rain all day and we'll be soaked to the skin. You better believe it."

"Well, let's hope not," she ventured timidly.

"Why should we hope anything? You're always hoping. Can't you see what's right in front of you?"

I waved my arm furiously at the crematoria, all of them ablaze, streaking the foggy night with huge leaping flames. In the glare we could see the fine rain beginning to fall, still so mingled with the mist that we didn't even feel it.

Lili kept silent and I didn't let out another word, just stood there feeling hostile and venomous, thinking of nothing in particular, transfixed by the garish flames against the dark sky.

As a rule, the Kommandos would start out late when it rained. We huddled against the barrack wall, seeking the illusion of shelter as we waited for it to grow light. Our dresses were soaked; the kerchiefs covering our hair dripped like leaky drainpipes; we shivered with cold as the loathsome damp seeped into our bones.

Finally we were ordered to start, and Mia, wearing a white plastic rain scarf, came to collect us for the review. As we neared the exit, we had a flicker of hope—part of the Kommando was being sent back. Maybe the officers would decide we couldn't work either. It would rain harder as the dreary day wore on; we'd have to go back inside the barrack and sit placidly on the straw mats waiting for our soup. I clutched at Lili's arm, the alluring prospect making me forget my ill humor. "Do you think maybe . . . ?"

But apparently our Kapo didn't share our notion of happiness. She was talking volubly to the officer in charge, who looked uncertain, listened, and at last signaled the Kommando to move on. Mia's eyes lit up: even on a day like today, she'd get to see her *kochany*.

Hunching down under the teeming rain, we marched to

the work site to find the trams full of water. And no matter how hard we tried, we couldn't dig up the wet sand. Even Mia was forced to recognize that work was literally impossible. For a while she stood at the door of the shack watching us struggle, then just as it began coming down in buckets, she decided to have us take refuge in the little chapel. It was too small to shelter the whole Kommando—a good number were left outside, jammed together on the stairs—but Lili and I were among the first to get in, packed so tight that we couldn't move a muscle. From the pressure of body heat, our wet clothes got wrung out and warmed, creating a cloud of humidity. When it stopped raining and cleared up, Mia came out of the shack to order us back to work, but called Lili aside and handed her the white sweater. So we returned to the trams while Lili sat down on the wet stairs of the chapel and, as before, bent diligently over her sewing.

"That little tramp has all the luck." Elenka, green with envy, gave her a snide look.

The path with the tracks was a muddy swamp by this time, making our clogs heavier with each trip, but there was no avoiding it. Also, the tram refused to budge—it simply slid around and got stuck in the mud.

"There he is!" Aërgi pointed to the sewage cart inching its way up the misty road, trailing the usual sickening smell.

This morning the Kapo sported a glossy raincoat. With his hands in his pockets, a cigarette in the corner of his mouth, he hurried toward the shack. As he passed by the chapel, he said something to Lili, who shook her head playfully, and then he disappeared inside.

Without the sun, the wearisome day stretched out interminably. Many of us had learned to pace ourselves by the sun's tracing its arc across the sky and had become so adept that we could tell precisely when the noon gong would sound, bringing the loaded *Esskolonne* (rations) truck. But with the overcast sky depriving us of our celestial clock, time stood still: one minute it would seem very early, and the next, almost time to head back. We were trapped in a gray, motionless world—truly Dante's "timeless" air in the circles of hell.

Some time after we had our soup, maybe close to three o'clock, the door of the shack opened and Mia's *kochany* came out, gazing around bemused, as though vaguely searching for something. It was obvious from his flushed face and glittery, slightly glazed eyes that he had had too much to drink. He took a step forward, then another, not quite sure where he was going, when his eye happened to light on Lili sitting on the chapel steps. Suddenly full of purpose, he went straight to her.

"Hey, little one," he boomed. "Hello there!"

From where I stood at my tram I could see Lili blush and look up in puzzlement at the massive figure planted before her.

"What is it?" she asked.

The fellow didn't bother to answer. He reached out to grasp her by the chin, forcing her to face him, and when she tried to pull away, he laughed and leaned over her.

"Oh, come on," he said, "what you so afraid of? You no want to be my *kochany*? Me and you, right?"

The whole Kommando had stopped work to watch. Again Lili tried uselessly to push him away, but he bent still closer, his lips brushing her neck. "You my *kochany*, okay?"

Just as he was kissing her, Mia appeared in the doorway.

For a split second she stared as if she couldn't believe what she was seeing, and then strode swiftly toward the chapel, her eyes shooting such daggers that even the drunkard could feel it. Scrambling back to his feet, he moved toward her with a forced smile. She ignored him and went right for Lili, who had backed up against the wall in an effort to shield herself. Mia snatched the sweater out of her hands, threw it in the mud, and proceeded to attack her.

None of us witnessed the beating. Mia's expression was so fearsome that we bent quickly over our shovels and began filling the cars with lightning speed. The sand flew from one shovel to another, heaping up and scattering, while only a few yards away this dreadful thing was happening. When at last the moaning and wailing ceased, Mia turned to us, her face crimson and murderous.

"Fill up those cars, you goddamned whores! You better fill them up if you know what's good for you."

She hurled herself on the nearest women, striking out on all sides like a whirlwind. I was gripped with the same terror as yesterday, when I waited for the blow and suffered in anticipation. But luckily I happened to be hidden by the tram, and by crouching as low as I could over the shovel, I kept out of sight and escaped the tempest.

Together we strained and pushed with nearly superhuman strength to move our immense load, for we had only one collective, screaming desire: to get away, to flee that unleashed madness. Helpless as we were, defenseless against Mia's violence, nothing but our lucky stars could save us.

As I pushed the tram along, I looked back and saw Lili lying flat on her face at the foot of the steps. She must have fainted. Just as well, I thought: that merciful temporary death was very often the best escape route from prolonged and ruthless beatings.

"Is she dead?" a woman next to me asked.

"Probably just passed out," I said and quickly stooped over the tram, for Mia was on the rampage again, brandishing her club. I caught a glimpse of her *kochany* behind her, all red in the face, smoking a cigarette and trying to grasp his beloved by the waist. She brushed him roughly aside and came toward us, shaking the club.

"Hurry up! Fill those trams up good! Be quick about it!"

All that day she tormented us. There wasn't a second to catch our breath. The loads of sand sped by one after the other but were never heaped high enough to satisfy her. She followed us up to the road and back to the quarry, giving us no relief from her presence. On one of our return trips we saw Lili digging at our mound of sand.

Poor Lili. Her apron was gone. Her dress, so carefully mended, was in shreds. Blood streaked down her swollen face, her shoulders, her legs. She saw me but didn't say a word when I went over. All I could think to do was touch her arm and murmur, "Oh, Lili."

"Leave me alone, Lianka." Her voice was barely audible.

I had to rush back to work because Mia had stationed herself right in front of our group. She waited until the car was full, and as we were about to lug it onto the tracks, she stepped forward.

"Five people for such a light load? That car's not even full. Anyone could move it with their bare hands. You, go ahead, let's see you try."

She was addressing Lili. The rest of us, dumbfounded at what Mia was demanding of her, moved aside as Lili obediently got a grip on the tram, bent over, and dug in her heels. Her veins bulged with the strain as her slight body pressed up against the mass of iron heaped with hundreds of pounds of sand.

"So you don't want to work, do you? You just want to be a whore." Mia glared at her with malice. "You want to lounge around and have a good time, eh?"

"I can't do it by myself, *Frau* Kapo," said Lili, again in that infinitely weary tone.

"You can't work? Well, that's tough luck, isn't it? That's your tough luck!"

And she spouted the camp's perennial slogan, which I had been hearing day in and day out for three months now, in every possible situation and inflection: "*Das ist ein Lager! Kein Sanatorium!* What about me? I've been in here five years! If I were as decrepit as all of you, I would have gone up in smoke long ago. But you, you all think you're here for some kind of rest cure. One smack and you burst into tears, two and you faint dead away—you can't even load a little sand onto a tram without whining about your breaking backs. You were all out there enjoying yourselves while we were rotting in the pouring rain. People were dropping dead left and right from the cold—you couldn't even take a step without tripping over them. This is a lager! Just look at these godforsaken creatures, here only a few months and they're half dead, they can't lift a finger, and they think they'll get home in one piece. You'll wind up in the crematorium, every last one of you, take my word for it. And it's what you deserve, because you're nothing but a bunch of filthy whores, that's what you are!"

We listened in silence—a captive audience—until finally,

as if heaving up all her hate and scorn, Mia spit. And waving us back to our places, she withdrew into the shack.

It must have been late, almost quitting time, because Kommando 103 came by, which worked the farthest way off. Very soon, distant and muffled by the thickening mist, came the first stroke of the *Quarantänelager* gong.

It was as if a boulder rolled off our chests. The nightmarish day was actually drawing to a close. Three-quarters of an hour to get to the lager, an hour or so of roll-call if all went smoothly, a half-hour more to get settled—one way or another, in a couple of hours we'd be lying on our mats, far away from Mia, from the sand, the trams, the haunting fog. Freed into sleep. The ephemeral freedom of slaves, true, but freedom nonetheless.

The fog was dense, and before we were lined up to leave, the rain started falling in sheets. The second gong sounded, the tank cart came stumbling toward the lager, and the guard raced over to knock on the door of the shack.

The Kapo was out in a moment, pulling on his gloves. Behind him in the doorway stood Mia, gazing after him adoringly and clinging to his hand. "Till tomorrow," he called breezily over his shoulder.

"Till tomorrow," she called back. Evidently the storm had subsided; all was forgotten. He darted off with his guard, and an instant later they were up at the road, shouting at the men waiting at the bars: they were late, and roll-call was sacrosanct.

Mia came out again, wearing her waterproof scarf. "*Los!* Move it!" she yelled, and the column began marching swiftly and silently toward the lager, rain dripping from our soaked kerchiefs onto our faces. It was late, the twilight darkened by rain and fog. The whole world seemed nothing but fog, gloom, rain. Trudging along with my head bent, I thought of Lili Marlene's song:

> Carrying my burden through the mud and rain,
> Still I stagger onward, my head bowed down in pain.
> Whatever will become of me?

Whatever will become of me? I wondered, the mud splattering at my feet. Whatever will become of me? And of Lili, and all the rest? It wasn't so much the fear of death that pained me, but rather the galling futility of this existence suspended between two voids. Here today, gone tomorrow. What could be the point of all this suffering, bounded by parentheses, in the midst of nothing? Was it possible some God was looking down on me from above? Why did he put me here in the first place if I was simply to suffer and vanish without a trace? Had he no mercy, this God?

No, we could expect no mercy either in this world or beyond. We were alone, abandoned to our fate, with no one and nothing to ease our pain, not even the thought of our loved ones. They would mourn us, yes, but after a while they'd be smiling again:

> Maybe tonight you'll weep and sigh,
> But you'll be smiling by and by,
> For who, Lili Marlene?
> For who, Lili Marlene?

The song wrung my heart till I found myself in tears. I walked and I wept. Whatever will become of me? — and with each verse the tears stung more bitterly.

We were edging along the barbed wire fence of the *Qua-*

rantänelager, with Mia's *kochany* walking parallel to us on the other side as he did every day, and at a certain point she made us slow down so he could come closer for their parting rites. They looked greedily into each other's eyes across the space, slowly and lasciviously making sucking motions with their lips. When their farewell was completed, the Kommando resumed its marching pace. I still murmured the verses of "Lili Marlene," emblem of our hapless lot.

All at once the Kommando stopped short. Since we were practically at the lager gate, I was confused by this unscheduled stop. From the buzzing of the women up front, we gathered that something was up: another Kommando had been halted and was entering a few at a time.

"What is it? What's happening? An inspection? No, selection! Selection? Yes, yes, selection!"

The urgent voices rose in panic. No matter that all through the day these same women would raise their eyes to heaven and pray for their sufferings to be over. Now, with the end in sight, they were clutched with terror.

"Selection, Lianka," announced Aërgi with an air of resignation, like a dumb beast led off to the slaughter.

"Selection, it's a selection!" cried the skeletal Elenka, and she straightened her kerchief and briskly rubbed her face to bring some color to her ashy cheeks.

The women were frantically pulling themselves together, helping each other appear as alert and robust as possible. Aching backs straightened, held stiff by will; eyes brightened; cheeks turned rosy with violent pinching.

"Lili, fix yourself up a little," called Elenka, and to her sister she added, loud enough to be heard, "Today of all days, and just look at that face."

I tried to arrange Lili's hair and kerchief, but she pushed my hand away with defeat.

"Let me be, Lianka," she whispered, "it's a lost cause."

Not at all, I protested. She was only *kaputt* for the moment because Mia had beaten her, but normally she was stronger than Elenka or Aërgi or me. She couldn't just give up. When her turn came, she had to look unconcerned, so the doctor would see it was only a minor scuffle. She was seventeen years old—didn't she want to get home?

Lili merely shook her head, waving me away with that blighted gesture, like shooing away some nuisance. I could see it would do no good to insist. Turning back to observe the others, I was seized with rage. What was that idiotic Elenka crying about? Would she be so sorry to die? Was it pure fear, fear of vanishing into thin air, that made them all cling to this atrocious life? Yet they constantly swore they couldn't stand another minute.

We were getting closer; the first rows of our Kommando were at the gate. Now I could see the German doctor standing beside the officers, as well as Herna, the Slovak woman who served as his secretary and, it was rumored, his lover. With notebook and pencil in hand, he scrutinized the women filing in front of him, picking out any who looked wasted away. Herna would read out the number tattooed on the woman's arm, and he would write it down. Then the rows moved on, while the woman selected went to stand apart in a group of gradually increasing numbers, a group of the chosen. At night, in the crematorium truck, they would set forth on that long trip whose end Madame Louise had been unable to see.

A morbid curiosity snaked through the rows. Beyond even

fear and anticipation, the women shuddered with raw sensation.

"Did they take Iluska?" Rumors flew. "They took Esther!" And like spectators at a sports match, people craned their necks for a better view of the action on the field.

"Move along, you!" shouted our Kapo. Alongside the doctor, who was very tall and thin, Mia seemed to have shrunk to nothing.

As I came close, I concentrated above all on keeping in step—my mind was a blank. I did notice his hands, though: long, slender, very white. His pencil was poised in mid-air, ready to point to someone.

It was our turn. We marched up to the gate in time to the music's sprightly beat. Mengele's face, as he looked us over, was bland and impassive, with squinting little eyes, his figure rigidly erect in the impeccable uniform. The pencil was suspended in the air, not aimed at anyone in particular, when Mia stepped forward.

"This one, *Herr Doctor*." She pointed to Lili. "Always *kaputt*. She can't do the work."

"Out," the doctor said simply, waving the pencil at her.

And Lili stepped from the line. She held out her arm. Herna read off the number, and he wrote it down in his notebook.

Under Cover of Darkness

The new *blockowa*, apparently anxious to demonstrate who was boss, presented herself with her entire staff and began by having us line up in formation and stand rigidly at attention for some time as she strode among the ranks, barking out threats.

"Oh, *meine Damen*, you think you're something special because you come from lager B? Listen, I was in lager B for four years. As far as I'm concerned, you're all still in quarantine."

I was enraged at being separated from Stella and Jeannette and felt venomous toward this very young, well-dressed girl who paced menacingly back and forth, brandishing her whip. She wasn't the least bit attractive, but bony and sallow, totally lacking in any feminine grace or softness—the epitome of lager shrewdness, that cunning astuteness which in the space of four years had earned her the red band, the whip, and the goodwill of the Barracks Kapo.

The women around me were muttering in vexation. After all, we were from lager B, experienced workers, and now they dump us in this lousy, miserable lager A where we had spent the toughest period of quarantine. Considering our endless months in the camp you'd think we had the right to look down our noses at the new arrivals. And here we are right back with them!

When at last we were released—"Okay, get inside," Erna ordered—everyone made a mad dash for the narrow door, ready to pummel and trample over the others in order to get in first and grab a good place. There were close to four hundred women with the same idea, and since I wasn't among the strongest, I was constantly driven back. When I was finally permitted to enter, the good places were all taken, and even the not so good ones. The most I could hope for was something in one of the damp, dark crannies down at floor level, surrogate tombs, really. But even those were taken. Wherever I poked my head in I was turned away with hoots and insults: they already had five, six, seven people, there was no room, where did I plan to put myself?

"There's always room for one more in the crematorium!" a few women called out, shaking their fists and giving me nasty looks, till I was utterly sick at heart. It was frightening to think of spending the night on the damp bricks—if the *stubowa* caught me on the floor instead of on a mat she'd beat me—but I didn't know what else to do. I had already gone up and down all four aisles several times with no luck, but I kept roaming around in despair, just to do something, feeling more defeated and mortified with every step.

"Is there any room?" I asked at one of the last nooks.

"Yes," replied a voice from the shadows. "There's a space, if you want it."

This was so unbelievable that for a second I simply froze, then darted quickly in. What a relief! It was as if a great burden were suddenly lifted. The bunk was pitch dark and so damp that I could smell the rotting straw of the mat. But who cared? Now I had "my" place, I wouldn't have to spend the night on the brick floor, the *stubowa* wouldn't beat me: that alone was cause to rejoice.

"How many people are in here?" I asked my neighbor. It

was so dark I could barely see her, but she seemed rather fat, with a very pale moon-shaped face and a quiet, patient air. "She must be a good woman," I thought. And in fact she answered courteously, in broken German, that there were only two. No one wanted to sleep on the rotten mat; everyone who started out here eventually moved on to something better.

"What's the other one like?"

The fat girl made a face and tapped her forehead to indicate that our other bunkmate was a bit out of it, then added, as if by way of excuse, "She's old. She came here with her daughter, who was almost ready to give birth, so they sent her straight to the crematorium. The mother managed to pass. She seemed in good shape then, her hair was still black, but now she's *kaputt*. What happened with the daughter threw her off completely—the best thing is to pretend not to hear her."

A few minutes later Adela turned up, exactly as Maria had described her. She started squabbling over the bunk, the blankets, the mat, and addressed Maria in particular with a curious acrimony, glaring at her with surly black eyes as if she bore her a grudge for some specific and very grievous offense.

"She wants the whole space for herself," Adela grumbled, calling on me as witness to such appalling injustice. "The whole thing for her and her belly! But one of these days I'm going to tell Erna the whole story. You'll see, I'll go right to Erna."

Maria had so far said nothing, as if the old woman's outbursts didn't concern her, but now she lost patience. "Oh, tell her whatever you want, Adela," she said. "Say anything, but right now would you just stop yelling? And give the new girl a blanket—you have three."

"Me? I have three?"

Exasperated, the old woman turned around to me, clutching the blankets to her chest. But since I was involved this time, I spoke up heatedly. She couldn't keep everything in the bunk for herself—she'd better give me my share. When she refused, I resorted to force, shoving her up against the wall to make her give in. Then, having done battle for my blanket and won, I piled it on top of Maria's so we could both be warmer. I was freezing and deliberately stretched out against her soft, plump body. I felt warmer already and was convinced fate had come to my rescue. Yes, Maria was definitely going to prove a good bunkmate.

I didn't feel like sleeping yet, though. "How long have you been here?" I asked her. "Did you come alone?"

Maria had been in the camp for four months, she said, and had come alone, thank God. After quarantine she had been assigned to an inside Kommando that took care of the grounds behind the barracks, and so had remained in lager A. There was no extra bread on Wednesdays, but you could get out of work by mixing in with the crowd from quarantine, and that might be better in the long run. . . . Anyway, at this point . . .

"What do you mean, at this point? You too, eh? You think the war will be over by Christmas?"

"Of course it will," said Maria with serene confidence. "Even sooner—by Christmas we'll be back home."

She rolled over and said good night, but kept tossing and taking deep breaths as though she couldn't get enough air. Finally she got up, which was annoying—all that moving around let in the cold air under the blankets. I saw that old

Adela had gotten up too and was leaning out of the bunk to watch where Maria was going.

"She's sick again." She wheeled round to face me, as if letting me in on a major secret. "She has to get up every night."

I assumed Maria must have diarrhea and remarked that she'd be better off going to the infirmary, or at least eating a raw potato instead of the soup. It was common knowledge that raw potatoes were a good remedy for that. But Adela shook her head as if I was talking nonsense. For Maria's problem, she declared, raw potatoes wouldn't do a god-damned thing. As far as the infirmary, she'd sooner die than go there.

The old woman must really be off her head, I decided, and didn't answer. But she wouldn't leave me alone. Inching up closer, she murmured, "You know what's wrong with Maria? You want me to tell you?"

"What are you talking about?" I grunted sulkily. "Go back where you belong. I want to sleep."

"She's going to have a baby," the old woman said. "That's right, she's having a baby — she's a few months along. That's why she feels sick."

"A baby!" This was astounding. "How could she be having a baby? They would have done an abortion when she first got here. That's what they always do, everyone knows it."

"But they didn't realize," the old woman retorted, "and even now she manages to hide it. She's torn up the blankets and ties the strips around her stomach to flatten it. She works as if nothing's the matter. But I noticed, she can't put that one over on me. I know there's no way she could keep that fat belly here, like a *blockowa*, or that she can't get rid of her dysentery. I know all about babies. I had four of my own. I was about to become a grandmother when I was deported."

The words tumbled out hastily, as in her excitement, Adela edged up so close that her harsh, grim face was almost on top of me, making me cringe. I drew back from her stark black eyes and pretended indifference.

"So what? So let her be pregnant. If she's stupid enough to want to bring a baby into this world just to have it thrown in the furnace, that's her problem. I want to sleep, baby or no baby."

At the sound of Maria's footsteps I quickly moved away from the old woman: Maria had treated me kindly and I didn't want her to get the wrong impression, seeing me tête-à-tête with her enemy. She slid into the bunk, cold as ice, her legs sending shivers through me. She was breathing heavily, as if to shake off her illness.

"Do you feel sick?"

Maria mumbled something under her breath and stretched out in exhaustion. Every few minutes, though, she would shift around, still breathing with difficulty. I thought of what the crazy old woman had said. Maybe she was right after all, and Maria was actually pregnant. But what was the point of concealing it? Simply to have the baby at all costs? The more I pondered, the more her behavior seemed utterly selfish. Of course she wanted to give birth, it was an irresistible law of nature—but were the laws of nature still valid in a death camp? She refused to sacrifice her right to be a mother, refused the pain of having the child stripped from her, but why give birth to a creature who was doomed to feed the flames?

I went on theorizing in this vein, nursing a growing and supercilious contempt for this irrational mother, until I drifted off to sleep, coldly indignant at what I saw as her animal nature and gloating over my higher wisdom. The next time she got up and let the cold air slip in and spoil my cozy sleep, I was furious and rudely demanded to know if she planned to spend the entire night climbing in and out of bed.

When she said nothing, I didn't let up. "If you're sick, why don't you go to the infirmary? Well, why not? You'll get better and you won't make a nuisance of yourself." I slept very little that night, and dawn brought only more resentment.

The work in this new Kommando was boring, and I thought constantly of Stella and Jeannette: if I could only be with them, time wouldn't weigh so heavily. They used to tell me about their life in Paris and teach me slang and popular songs. If one of us had the thrill of discovering a bit of potato or carrot in the soup, we always divided it companionably in three parts. They were my true friends! Now I had to put up with this bovine Maria. In addition to everything else, she worked incessantly, never even trying to sneak away for a break. She would wield her hoe in a kind of trance, one stroke after another, with a silent, placid diligence that felt like a personal reproach.

Time and again I harassed her. "Why are you working so hard? Are you trying for a blue ribbon or something?" And when she responded with a mild shrug, as if to say working helped pass the time, the other girls would chime in with their cheap abuse: she must have plenty of energy if she loved working so much. Too bad the rest of us didn't have all that fat to work off! But we had no *protekcja* (special privileges), not us, we couldn't even get enough to fill our bellies.

They would taunt her ever more crudely, pleased at any

momentary distraction from the work, till in the end I recoiled in shame from their weary eyes gleaming with malice and their pinched mouths spewing out vulgarities, sick at the sight of what our misery had made of us. I felt bitter remorse for tormenting someone weaker than I, yet in some ways so much stronger. I could have wept at my own brutality. Soon I would be a true daughter of the lager: my mouth would mold itself into a thin, cruel line, the lips twisted in a scornful grimace. I would be no different from the old-timers. And I admonished myself, softened my heart. I got close to Maria again and tried to show her kindness.

"Why are you always so quiet?" I asked.

Maria shook her head and gave her meek smile. She had nothing especially interesting on her mind, she said. She was forever thinking of home. Oh, blessed home! How long, oh Lord, how long? I didn't understand German very well, and she spoke it with a mixture of the Yiddish dialect that to my ears was the most hideous language on earth. Nevertheless I gathered, in bits and pieces, that Maria came from a small provincial city. When the Germans came, she had been married only a short time and had barely gotten the house in order, four rooms and a garden. . . . She liked flowers, but her region was cold, it was hard to grow them. In the sunniest part of the garden there was a grapevine that gave little clusters, but they never grew quite plump or ripe enough. . . . She was good at canning and pickling: when the SS trooped into the house, the kitchen shelves were lined with lovely gleaming jars of pickles, jams, syrups for winter. She had prepared them all so lovingly. She wondered who carried them off.

"I'll have to do it all over again," she sighed. I carefully refrained from any comments or conjectures that might dash her hopes.

Thus Maria stopped being an abstract figure to be judged by abstract reasoning. She was no longer a selfish monster but a warm, good, trusting human being, and I had all the sympathy in the world for her. For all I knew, if I were pregnant I might have felt the same, might have trusted that the war would be over before the nine months were up and that my baby would lie in a white cradle, in a white room. . . . Of course, I would have felt exactly the same!

And so I renounced my ill will and brutishness. For one thing, I inevitably got used to the idea. And then, by imagining myself in her predicament, I couldn't help but feel for her. I would stay close by as we worked on the grounds behind the barracks, and one day I took a good look at her face: how sad and wan, with grayish blotches and deep circles under the eyes. I asked her age and was shocked: just twenty-three.

"Twenty-three!" I must have looked so incredulous that Maria couldn't help noticing.

"Back home I didn't look like this," she said, shaking her head in her usual way, with such a profoundly resigned melancholy that my heart went out to her; it was almost the way you feel for a beloved pet who suffers in all innocence. I tried to distract her with frivolous chatter: she had such beautiful hair, such lovely dark eyes and thick, arched eyebrows—did she wear a lot of mascara back home?

I rattled on, but Maria didn't answer. At first I paid no attention, but when I finally turned around, I was alarmed.

"What's the matter? Don't you feel well?"

She motioned that I should keep still, then sank to the

ground, her hands supporting her stomach. White as a sheet, her forehead beaded with sweat, she was writhing with the effort to conceal how sick she felt. Each time I came close and tried to help, she waved me away in terror.

"They'll see you," she whispered. "Go away, I'm afraid they'll notice. It's passing; I'm getting up. . . . As long as they don't realize . . . Go on, go. . . ."

Don't realize what? I asked. Maria raised her head. As if she could no longer bear the double anguish of suffering and secrecy, she looked me straight in the eye. So it's true? I asked wordlessly. It's true, her eyes replied, and she bowed her head and wept. As I reached out to stroke her cheek, she trembled and pressed my hands to her mouth. I felt them grow damp with her tears.

"My poor, dear Maria," I said over and over. Everything would be all right, I assured her. It would all turn out fine.

I remembered to keep an eye out all the while and noticed a German approaching—the middle-aged little brunette who went around with a huge German shepherd. Her ashen face was cold and sealed; she would never beat anyone on a mere whim, as our Kapos often did, but once she got started she didn't relent until the unfortunate victim lay bloody and unconscious at her feet.

"Watch out," I whispered, grabbing the pickaxe. Maria hastily got to her feet and resumed her hoeing as if nothing had happened, and by the time the German reached us we were hard at work. With a frozen stare, she paused as if to let us know she had seen us sitting down. She said nothing, though, and after what was probably just a few moments but felt like an eternity, she left. As soon as she disappeared behind the barrack I got all excited.

"How far along are you?"

"Today I entered my seventh month."

With that the ice was definitely broken. But first Maria made me solemnly swear not to tell a soul her dangerous secret.

"If anything happens to me, it'll be on your conscience," she warned.

I certainly wouldn't go around gossiping, I reassured her. Anyway, who would I tell? Old Adela?

"Especially not her. You mustn't breathe a word to her, remember," Maria urged. "She's hated me ever since she figured it out, because her own daughter was killed. She was almost in her ninth month when she got here, so they didn't even let her in the camp. Adela can't stand the idea that someone else is going to get away with it, that my baby'll be born when the war is over and we'll both go home. She's all alone and knows very well that with her gray hair she doesn't stand a chance of getting home. Sooner or later she'll be picked in a selection. She once said to me, 'You really think you're going to get away with this, you think you'll make it to the end? You'll see, God will take care of you the same way he took care of my daughter. If he didn't let her baby see the light of day, why should he do any different for yours? What did you ever do to deserve special favors? Oh sure, you've made it this far because they didn't realize and do an abortion, but even if you carry it to term it'll be labor in vain. They'll just take the baby from you and throw it straight in the oven without even bothering with the gas. It'll all be a lot of trouble for nothing, all your labor.'"

"Adela told you that?" I felt so sorry for Maria. Her eyes brimmed with tears, and she seemed terribly upset and worn out. "Well, it's not written in stone. When are you due?"

In about two months, she said.

"Ah, but in two months it'll all be over. So what are you crying about, silly?" I gave her a hug, totally convinced that kind-hearted nurses would hold the baby in their arms and lay it in a white cradle.

"This baby has to have the best of everything, because he made it through the lager, right?" Maria echoed. She brightened up at the notion of the cradle and let herself revel in the warm aura of motherhood, confident that in the space of two months we would be welcomed into a new world, a world of love and mercy, where everyone who suffered under the smoke of Birkenau would be blissfully happy. As for me, it was the same old story: I couldn't help being drawn in, though I was well aware that this was no more than the loveliest of illusions, while reality itself would be another thing entirely. In no time at all I was thoroughly caught up in her vision of the happiness to come.

Once entrusted with Maria's secret, I came to realize how much she must have suffered and endured, with the heroic obstinacy of a martyr, for the cherished life throbbing inside her. She continued to work with the same self-effacing attitude, spurring herself on, unlike the rest of us, so as to avoid any possible suspicion. If anyone happened to glance curiously at her slightly rounded stomach, she would start and turn pale, with a faint, irrepressible tremor of the lips.

The days dragged by. Having come from a much worse Kommando, I didn't find the work a great strain. I could stay awake in the evening and be sociable instead of promptly collapsing in exhaustion like a dead weight. I would lie down next to Maria and listen to her gentle voice murmuring phrases of hope and expectation: every passing day was one more triumph over those who controlled our destiny; every day strengthened her faith in the divine providence whose help she never doubted.

And so I too let myself be lured into certainty that the war would soon be over. My own life seemed to merge with the two lives beside me; my more lucid convictions slipped away, and I fell into the enchanting deception, like soothing, beguiling child's play.

"What shall we name it?" I asked one evening. "You want a girl, don't you? We have to choose a really pretty name."

Maria hadn't thought about that yet, and so we went through all the possible names and finally agreed on "Erika." Graced with a name, the unborn child gradually took over our lives. I was solemnly proclaimed the future godmother. I would be far away, of course, and could visit my goddaughter only on rare occasions, but Maria promised to keep me meticulously informed of her every move.

"When she's grown up, she can read my books!" I said, swept away by enthusiasm. "Maybe in a few years I'll write her a fable about how a wicked stork carried her off and wanted to drop her in a terrible place called a lager, but I knew this stork and after many adventures I made the stork bring her to a room with a white crib all ready for her. And that's how Erika came to sleep in a feather bed instead of on a straw mat."

"Oh no." Maria smiled. "That way you'll get all the credit. Write that you let the stork drop her in the lager."

More than once during these whimsical conversations I caught Adela staring at us with a mad, shifty look. Surely the old woman had feelings too. One time when Maria had gone to the garbage heap—she had a craving for squash skins—I went over to her. Each day she seemed to sink deeper into her mute, desolate hostility. Perhaps I could show some understanding.

She was hunched up in a corner, voraciously eating a salad of a sort, made from the little herbs that grew at the edge of the camp and sprinkled with a bit of yellow mustard the girls from the kitchen sold for a few slices of bread. She looked up and instinctively clutched her bowl to her chest as if my appearance threatened violence or theft.

"What are you afraid of, Adela?" I said, addressing her politely for the first time: I had resolved to treat her as a human being. She made a wry face, as if to say, "you never know," and went on eating in silence.

"It would be nice to have a piece of bread with that," I remarked, simply to say something. "Those greens with mustard on a nice slice of bread—that would be delicious. I love mustard. At home I always put it on pot roast. Do they use it a lot where you come from?"

She mumbled an assent. Now that our talk had taken a culinary turn it was easier to go on, and Adela too was responding and getting interested, to the point of telling me that actually she didn't do very much cooking.

"Neither do I. Maybe you were able to hire a good cook, though?"

"No," she said. "My daughter did the cooking."

The words were clipped, as though held in check by some particular reserve. She immediately grew sullen again.

"My daughter did all the cooking," she repeated, paying no more attention to me. "She was the one who could cook." And she stared off into space, perhaps seeing the image of the beloved face. She started mumbling to herself and shaking her head, her dark sunken eyes wide open, the pupils dilated, fixed on that obscure point where her young daughter, dead before her time, must have been smiling at her across the space.

I had heard the old woman was a widow and had only that one daughter left. They had journeyed here together, but they weren't released together in the black, dissolving smoke of Birkenau. Fate really twisted the knife with Adela, I thought ruefully. Here she manages to survive and drag herself along through every outrage and atrocity, while the two young lives that were all she treasured on earth were taken first.

I remembered what Jeannette used to say, watching the dense spirals rise from the crematoria and trail across the sky: the black curls were the souls of the lager's old-timers, marching in orderly rows of five toward the kingdom of the merciful God, while the wispy little white curls that drifted and vanished waywardly, the merest puffs, were the souls of children and newcomers who had yet to learn discipline. Adela's daughter and future grandchild had drifted off that way, still astonished, floating in the sky like dancers, but the old woman would go up in the thick smoke of an old-timers' selection, a pitiable end. I was humbled and remorseful, and felt I must try to know Adela better. Maria was a good, sweet girl; youth and hope together would give her courage, but this solitary old woman, destined to die alone and uncomforted, must be in far greater pain.

"What are you thinking about, Adela?" I asked. She had the bowl resting on her knees as if she had lost interest. "Don't you want to finish your salad?"

She roused herself brusquely and caught me looking greedily at it. "You want it? Here, eat!" And she flung the bowl in my lap.

Shamefaced, I refused. Anyway, who could trust such

undreamed of luck? But Adela repeated the offer in the same surly tone and, without another word, turned her back and shrank into a corner of the bunk. I knew it would be only right to show some concern for her, especially as I had provoked this explosion of grief. And yet . . . the tingle of the mustard on my tongue, the taste of a few crumbs dipped in watery salad dressing—my craving was more powerful than any merciful impulse. I hurriedly got the bit of bread I had left over and avidly wiped up every drop of the precious dressing.

"I'll leave a little for Maria," I thought at one point, but the frenzy of eating won out. I kept scraping at the bowl long after the greens and dressing were gone, until the aluminum bottom gleamed as if it had been scoured with pumice-stone and hot water.

Only then did I remember Adela, curled up in the corner under the blanket. I felt guilty for neglecting her. I moved closer and heard her talking to herself but couldn't make out what she said. The words were interspersed with spasms of weeping, and every few minutes she stopped to wipe her nose on the blanket.

"Adela," I murmured, but she didn't respond. I patted her gently on the shoulder. "Adela, what is it?"

She still didn't answer; but she didn't push me away either. I moved closer, fighting my disgust. She was just a heap of bones draped in rags. Finally she turned around, and I could only pity her: her eyes were red and blurred with tears, yet her gaunt, wrinkled ruin of a face kept a trace of its once delicate contours.

"What do you want?" she whispered. I stammered something she must have understood as a clumsy desire to comfort her, and she shook her head. "It's no use. What can you say to me?"

All at once she sat bolt upright, her mood and expression transformed, as though she still couldn't accept her fate. Her eyes shot out sparks of rebellion, as well as infinite loathing.

"It's not fair! It's just not fair! Why should my poor daughter die with her innocent baby who never even got to open his eyes, and others don't? What harm did she ever do? And the baby, not born yet, what crime did it commit? How can they say there's a God? And I have to watch that goddamned bitch wrap up her belly every morning so no one sees she's pregnant! She gets away with it too, and what did the two of them ever do to deserve it? Both of you lie there all night picking out names and talking nonsense. You talk low, but do you think I can't hear you? Even if you didn't say a word I would know what you're thinking! Damn you too! Give me that!"

She snatched the bowl from my hands. Just then I saw Maria returning and darted back to my corner to cut short this dreadful scene.

"What were you fighting about with Adela?" She stretched out wearily on the mat. Her stomach was getting rounder and more noticeable; I had to help her bind it up every morning.

"Oh, the usual rubbish." I glanced at Adela from the corner of my eye. She was looking daggers at us but said nothing, so I began jabbering to Maria about something or other. I could still feel that glare, though, and it gave me a weak, sick feeling. Each time I stole a look in her direction she was still crouched with the empty bowl on her lap, eyes wide with menace, head nodding, muttering phrases that must have been pounding in her skull.

"What did she say to you?" Maria asked again when we were huddled under the blankets. "Something about me?"

I didn't want to lie or admit the truth, so I just mumbled that she was getting crazier all the time.

"The way she watches us with those eyes! She'd be glad to see me dead," said Maria. "But Erika wants to see the snow this winter. . . ."

"Do you get much snow in your parts?" I asked. And Maria began describing how cold it got, how there was lots of snow, but it stayed nice and warm inside with the big heating stoves and the fireplaces going. She'd make sure to put Erika's cradle in a warm, snug place so she didn't catch cold.

We got so involved in our talk, she recalling the Moravian winter and I the winter on the Riviera, that I forgot all about Adela and her mad eyes. I was on the verge of sleep when Maria shook me. "It's a holiday tonight," she said softly. "Hanukkah. Do you want to come see?"

She was sitting up, putting on her clogs. I hadn't the least desire to move and said as much, but she kept urging me until I agreed to come along.

There was a rare hush in the barrack, for all the Hungarian Jews, who were the majority of its occupants, had gathered in the corridor opposite a small room where, from time immemorial, sinks were being installed. The ladies of the Block had brought in a table covered by a gleaming white tablecloth. On either side stood a small vase filled with wildflowers, the kind the field Kommandos would respectfully present to the barracks Kapos, and in the center, on a little tray with oil, were arrayed the eight slender candles symbolizing resistance and victory. The Block Kapo, holding a tiny, crumpled book, loudly chanted the ancient prayers as the women echoed them in chorus.

"Look!" said Maria, her eyes lit with joy. "Isn't it beautiful?"

The *blockowa* touched a match to the first candle.

It caught, flickered, and as the women chanted the hymn of thanksgiving, imploring the fearful and almighty God to keep the flame of their faith eternally lit through century after century of grief, destruction, and persecution, it glittered with a splendid light.

"Next year we'll be lighting them at home," the women whispered, their bright eyes fixed on the little flame.

But one woman, overcome with the emotion stirred up by memories, burst into tears. Wailing with grief, she named all the names of those who would not see the sacred candles lit next year, nor the year after, nor ever again, for any holiday on earth. One after another, the women took up her cries, and soon nearly everyone was sobbing in desolation, while the *blockowa* and a handful of others went on intoning their faith in a just God.

"Let's go," I said to Maria.

She stepped reverently to the improvised altar and, bowing her head, gazed down at the flickering, gleaming flame. I knew she was envisioning next year, when she would stand in front of her ancient Menorah holding little Erika in her arms, straining a bit under her weight, and give thanks for the emblematic light; the dismal barrack at Birkenau would be but a shadowy, long-gone dream.

"Thank you, Lord, for rescuing me," she would murmur. "You thank him too, little one. Thank God for sparing your life."

Yes, this would all come to pass. I could read it in Maria's fervent eyes, could hear it in the imploring voices of those who prayed, and even in the laments of the women embracing each other, recalling their loved ones who were lost and their own uncertain fates.

"Lord, have mercy on us. Grant us salvation, oh Lord. Watch over us, almighty God."

At last they began drifting off. But on the way many paused to look out the narrow little window that let a bit of air into the barrack.

"Look how it's burning! Good God, just look at that fire! What's going to become of us, this holiday?"

Maria and I paused too. The night sky was crimson and spangled with enormous flames rising ceaselessly from the crematorium smokestacks, surrounding the camp with a lofty ring of fire visible from far off—from the houses in Auschwitz, the peasant cottages, the distant villages.

What could they all be saying? "What huge fires at Birkenau tonight! It's the Jewish holiday. They must be having bonfires to commemorate it."

The flames rose high enough to light up every path in the camp. Reflections of flame danced in the mud and the puddles, on the gray barrack roofs, on the pained faces of the women who watched in silence.

"Come on, Maria," I begged. She seemed entranced, unable to tear herself away. "Come, it's late and we have to work tomorrow."

But she leaned her head out, as if straining her ears.

"Do you hear?" she whispered. "Do you hear the Polish women in Barrack 4 singing?"

I listened—yes, there was a faint, muffled sound of voices singing. Again all the women paused to listen to the song of long-suffering, dogged hope, and in a kind of mystical rapture, echoed it, their faces glimmering in reflections of flame consuming perhaps the very people they were dreaming of moments ago, the loved ones they would rejoin next year to light, in freedom, the eight slender candles.

The altar, the prayers, the lugubrious spectacle of a sky lit bright as day by human flesh ablaze, the echo of that excruciatingly sad song all left me overwrought. Without a word to Maria I went back to my mat, where I glimpsed a face retreat furtively in the shadows. Adela was pretending to be asleep, while most likely she had been out of the bunk, spying on the ceremony.

A little later Maria returned, still quivering with emotion. "Next year in freedom," she said with a tremor, then kissed me good night and lay down.

No one got right to sleep that night, though. Every few minutes someone else broke out in uncontrollable sobbing, until it seemed the entire barrack would lapse into mass hysteria and Erna had to come to restore silence: it was late, didn't we realize we had to work the next day? With my eyes closed, I lay tense in a stubborn determination to fall asleep, distracted by Adela moving restlessly in her corner. What an ordeal this evening must have been for her, I thought: she could offer God nothing but reproach.

Maria, however, breathed easily. She slept on her back, hands crossed on her stomach at long last free from restraints; her face was serene, as if she had fallen asleep with some sweet, consoling vision.

"Can't you sleep, Adela?" I asked. The old woman wouldn't stop tossing about, muttering to herself. "What's the matter, don't you feel well?"

She didn't answer, so I turned back toward Maria and

tried to will myself to sleep. But distant childhood memories
kept surging up. I saw my grandmother's milky white hand
at the brass Menorah, lighting one candle after another, up
to the seventh. The eighth was saved for me. She picked me
up in her arms so I could reach it. And then? What happened then?

Ah, then my grandfather gave me a kiss. He had a white
mustache and blue eyes full of tenderness. Oh, grandpa,
grandpa, why am I in Birkenau?

So I fell asleep at last and woke only when our *stubowa*
yanked me by the feet, hurling away the covers and yelling
that it was my turn to fetch the coffee. "Up, get up! *Aufstehen! Kaffee holen!*" she shouted with idiotic persistence,
refusing to shut up until I put on my shoes. Maria and Adela
were on duty too, which didn't help matters, since Adela
had no strength and Maria was very slow. I was hardly looking forward to carrying the incredibly heavy iron vat with the
two of them plus some fourth person, depending on the luck
of the draw.

"This is going to be a rough trip," I said to Maria under
my breath.

She nodded. "My back hurts so this morning, I can't even
stand up straight."

In the meantime Adela had dashed off somewhere. She
had already played that trick more than once, leaving us to
be berated by the escort *stubowa*. I was furious.

"Take it easy," Maria advised. "Let's just go." I followed
her unwillingly. Fetching the coffee or soup from the kitchens was to me one of the nastiest chores in the lager, and I
would gladly have done without the murky, insipid brew that
changed color—dark when it tried to pass for coffee, lighter
when it was labeled tea.

The others were just starting to dress, while we stood at the entrance to the kitchens, sullen and shivering in the lager's chill silence. Waiting on the dark road, we glanced over "there," where a few tongues of flame still rose and played, as if last night's festivities were reluctant to come to an end. From the kitchens came laughter and lighthearted voices, as through the half-open door we glimpsed that fabled realm — warm, with plenty to eat — where the women were round and rosy, nicely dressed, full of merriment. I was willing to bet those girls in the kitchen never worried about how they'd get through another year.

"Get moving, you!" shouted the *stubowa*, and so we did, along with two women who were recruited at the last minute and quickly grabbed the best positions.

"Up we go," said Maria. We each gripped a handle as I stood behind her with my free hand on her back, to push her along. This was the classic lager method of carrying the vats, and demanded a certain coordination of pace and energy, so as not to lurch about wildly with your back about to break any minute.

Needless to say, each of us wanted to exert ourselves as little as possible and tried to shift the burden onto the others. Every so often the vat would rock and sway, the boiling liquid would spill onto our hands, and we would have to stop and change positions, with mutual accusations of carelessness and malingering. This morning we had to stop even more than usual — virtually every minute — because Maria, despite all her efforts, couldn't hold up her end of the vat. The other two women cursed and complained.

Maria winced as she straightened her back.

"Are you in a lot of pain?"

"Yes, it's pretty bad."

I was getting worried. We had quite a ways to go before we reached our Block, and the Kommandos were starting to line up. We would definitely be the last to arrive, and all the *stubowas* would be up in arms. God help us if we met an auxiliary along the *Lagerstrasse*, or even worse, the *Lagerkapo*, Maria la Morte! As fate would have it, when we got to the corner of our Block, her tall figure suddenly loomed up: "What's this! You didn't bring the coffee yet?" she shrieked. "It's time for roll-call and you're still carrying the coffee?"

She raised her club. The blow got me between the shoulders like a streak of fire through my flesh, knocking the breath out of me. The women in our Block were lined up outside watching the scene with interest, for the *Lagerkapo* on the rampage always provided an element of spectacle, the thrill of the arena.

"Move it, quick, you lazy good-for-nothings! I'll teach you how to carry coffee!" she screamed, driving us forward with blows of her club. We naturally went as fast as we could, stumbling and tottering; our gait took on the staggered rhythms of a fugue played against the club. We had almost made it to the door of the Block when Maria tripped and fell over on her back, and the vat, tilted off balance, overturned and spilled out on the road.

"What are you doing, you goddamned bitches? What's going on?" Erna hollered, running over.

Luckily, the *Lagerkapo* had rounded the corner before Maria fell, leaving us only the *blockowa* to deal with, which was something of a relief. Erna was on top of us, striking out frantically. Maria lay on the ground, pale as a ghost, her eyes closed, as Erna kicked her again and again, shouting insults and curses. The repeated kicking made the edge of Maria's dress slide up, revealing a strip of blanket.

Erna's sharp eyes spotted it immediately. She seized it and tugged violently, dragging Maria several feet along the ground as the strip lengthened in her hands.

"What's this! What is it? Aha! The fine lady is afraid of getting a chill in her stomach! Madame likes her comforts," Erna yelled sarcastically, clutching the incriminating strip and shaking it furiously.

I had taken my place in line and looked on with my heart in my throat. Maria just lay there as the *blockowa* yanked at the strip of blanket, poking her with the tip of her foot.

"Wearing a corset so you don't catch cold, eh? Some fancy lady, she watches out for her own skin, doesn't she? Just get a load of them, fat enough to burst, and they can't carry a little pail of coffee. They come tumbling down like rotten apples."

"Maria is pregnant, *Frau blockowa*," came a voice out of the blue. Erna spun around, every head turned, and Adela found herself the focus of a unanimous and passionate curiosity. She stood surrounded, cool as a cucumber, frowning slightly.

"Pregnant?" Erna repeated incredulously. "She's pregnant? How do you know? What kind of crazy story is that?"

"She's pregnant, *Frau blockowa*. Every morning she binds her belly up tight to make it flat. I sleep next to her, I'm telling the truth, believe me."

"It's true," whispered a girl next to me. "I saw her do it too. I knew what she was up to. Remember that night she kept us all up?"

And suddenly everyone was whispering, everyone had

known the truth about Maria all along. In the meantime Adela had stepped forward as if she feared the accused might make a run for it, while Erna, upset and perplexed, seemed at a loss and whispered nervously to her clerk and the other *stubowas* gathered around. Maria got back up on her feet. She stroked her stomach and made fumbling efforts to straighten out her clothes as she gazed, bewildered, at Adela and the *blockowa*.

"Is it true you're pregnant?" asked Erna.

She blushed and hesitated, unable to come up with an answer. Still stroking her swollen belly, she looked straight at the informer. The old woman stared back, stubborn and implacable, stiff with the willfulness of the accuser—a wretched figure, radiating such intense hatred that Maria seemed crushed. She averted her eyes and nodded timidly.

"So you're really pregnant!" Erna exploded. "You have some nerve putting it over on us all this time. Don't you know if you're pregnant you have to say so right off, in quarantine? How many times did the nurses tell you? So why didn't you let anyone know? Why, you prize whore! Why!"

All during the *blockowa*'s beating Maria had lain mute and motionless, resigned to her fate, knowing how useless it would be to fight back. Now that she was addressed directly, however, she wrenched herself out of her passivity, raising her head with an air of decision and looking calmly back at Erna.

"Because I didn't want an abortion," she replied. "I knew they did abortions on the women in their first few months, so I decided not to tell and just keep going. . . ."

"Will you listen to this!" yelled Erna, more furious than

ever. "This lady didn't want an abortion. Better to give birth to the little brat and send some more smoke up the chimney, right? Well, I don't give a damn about that! All I know is that your goddamned brat is going to be one big pain in the ass—that's all I care about! How far along are you? Answer me!"

"Seven months," Maria whispered.

The *blockowa* was absolutely scandalized.

"Seven months! This whore is walking around here with a seven-month belly! And what am I supposed to do now? Four years in the lager and they'll tell me I still don't know how to be a *blockowa* if some slut can pull this on me. I'll wind up caught in the middle! Me! Me!"

This was the one thing that obviously unhinged her, for she suddenly turned on Adela, who had stood silently the whole time, not moving a muscle, staring like a lunatic at Maria's hands grazing her aching stomach.

"You knew all about it! You should have told me! Why did you wait till now, you old idiot? Oh why, why didn't they send you to the crematorium!"

She hurled herself on Adela and sent her rolling on the ground. The old woman seemed hardly to notice: she merely got up, smeared with mud, and proceeded to shake out her dress. Defiant, triumphant, she never took her eyes off Maria.

The Block clerk, a shrewd, slippery little Polish woman who looked like an eternally hunted animal, returned carrying her register and took Erna aside to confer. She had apparently come up with a good idea, for Erna's face relaxed as she listened and nodded, yes, yes, very good, that sounded fine. The clerk went over to Maria.

"At roll-call, you'll stay in the last row from now on, you understand? And you're switching Kommandos—you're not working outside anymore. You'll work in the Block, get it? You'll only go out to get water and empty the buckets at night."

We had all assumed Maria would be sent to the infirmary, and so this highly propitious solution left us stunned. In no time, a hiss of whispered commentary erupted. Maria was the object of curiosity, envy, suspicion. It just takes luck, people muttered peevishly. All a matter of luck. Some people have all the luck.

I turned to Adela. The old woman's face was a study in confusion and anguish. As if she couldn't believe her ears, she began running to catch up with the clerk and the *block-owa* as they walked off.

"But she's pregnant," she said over and over in the insistent, monotonous rhythm of the crazed. "She's pregnant, I'm telling you."

Erna and the clerk wheeled around angrily, but then as Adela wouldn't stop, they burst out laughing.

"Okay, okay, so she's pregnant. Do you want to be too? Would you like that?"

They were still laughing when they began counting the women. Maria went to the last row, and by the time the auxiliary arrived for inspection, the only trace left of the entire incident was a large dark stain on the ground, where the coffee had spilled.

I spent the rest of that day alone; Maria stayed behind in the barrack and I couldn't get to see her. She was, however, the subject of interminable discussions, since the revelation of the pregnancy was the major event of the day. All the

women were vehemently critical: they couldn't seem to for-
give her for trying to escape the common fate and considered, as I had done, that her optimistic love for the unborn
child was arrogant to the point of madness. There was also
a good deal of comment on the clerk and the *blockowa's*
extraordinarily benign stance. One old-timer called Elenka,
who always welcomed the opportunity to say something
unpleasant, mumbled that there was more here than met
the eye. We could rest assured the *blockowas* weren't about
to risk their necks to save Maria's kid. No, something was
definitely fishy about such strange and unprecedented tol-
erance. That foxy old clerk must have figured out a way to
get rid of the problem.

I didn't set any store, at first, by Elenka's remarks. And
yet every evening I found Maria looking more exhausted and
downtrodden. I began to think it over and to worry. There
she was, consigned to isolation, cut off from the shared work
of the group; most likely Erna and her acolytes were deliberately wearing her down day by day with their brutal treatment. Worse than wrecking her body, this could destroy her
spirit.

The only place she could find any peace was in our bunk,
for Adela had moved: we were rid of the haunting, hateful
eyes. She slept alone in a hole so dark and damp that no
one else would dare stay in it. In the evenings she sat huddled
on her mat, despondent, embittered, from time to time shaking her head in the gesture that was part and parcel of her
obsession. At this point most of the girls called her "crazy
lady" and mocked her, some going so far as to parade in
front of her with their stomachs puffed out.

"I'm having a baby, Adela," they jeered with their coarse

hilarity. And the old woman would peer out in puzzlement, then grow angry as they continued to taunt her, trying to provoke her with great guffaws of laughter.

"I'm having a baby, didn't you know? Why don't you go tell Erna? I'm having two, Adela! For me you better go to the *Lagerkapo!*"

They carried on until the old woman flew into a rage and began hurling things at them, anything within reach. Then they would go off laughing, satisfied with their cruel pranks.

I had not greeted her since that notorious morning and simply ignored her whenever I passed her nook, for Maria had made me promise not to give her a hard time.

"It's hopeless," she would say with a sigh. This was unlike her, and I found those words on her lips quite unnerving: I had grown used to finding hope through her hope. It was only through her trusting nature that I could harbor the precious illusions my reason haughtily refused to indulge.

"What on earth are they doing to you?" I asked one evening as she tossed fretfully. "You were in better shape when you worked outside."

"Outside!" she exclaimed in an agonized, quivering voice. "Outside was paradise! If you only knew, Liana, what it is to lug the sleeping mats around for an entire day, and wash the floor dozens of times over, then just when you think you're done, a *stubowa* comes along and dumps pails of garbage on it and starts kicking you and saying you must have grown up in a stable. Plus hauling buckets of water and sacks of bread and straw . . . All day long they rack their brains trying to find ways to kill me, all in a day's work, you know, no scandal. That's why they had me stay in the Block. Sure, if we can manage to get rid of them for good, they think, her and her little brat, everything'll be back to normal, no more headaches. That's all they want. What a fool I was to think I could make it out of Birkenau, that this innocent child could open her eyes among human beings, not these barbarians. But it's all been wasted effort, all these months of torture for absolutely nothing. They'll win in the end, and there's not a thing I can do about it. I only pray to God to get it over with fast, because I can't go on anymore. I can't take another minute of this."

Maria fell back on the mat and sobbed. What could I say? She had struggled against fate and been crushed, totally undone. Her life would come to nothing. I would never bring my godmother's gift to little Erika. I thought grudgingly of Adela. Yes, if she knew how her enemy wept and suffered, no doubt she'd be very gratified.

"Oh, God in heaven," Maria moaned, pressing her face into the mat. It was a timorous, irrepressible cry of rebuke, uttered in fright and dismay. She had been ready and willing to submit to God's unfathomable decrees, and now she was lost, abandoned to cruelty and torment. "Lord, what did I ever do? What did we do? What crime did this poor unborn child ever commit?"

In the midst of all this, Erna came over and ordered her to fetch the coffee from the kitchen.

"How can I, *Frau blockowa?*" she said softly, pointing to her swollen legs. "I can hardly stand on my feet."

She could stand up fine, Erna snarled, when it came to drinking it. Just who did she think she was anyway?

"*Das ist ein Lager!*" Once again, the perennial slogan. "*Das ist ein Lager, kein Sanatorium!*"

She tried to get her up, but with a boldness inspired by

desperation, Maria resisted and clung to the mat. Erna pulled mightily to yank her up, then kicked her hard two or three times. One kick must have landed in her stomach, because Maria let out a shriek and clutched herself with both hands. She broke out in a sweat and fell back down, her face gray and contorted with pain.

"I'll go get the coffee," I shouted at Erna. "Leave her alone, can't you see she's sick?"

She told me to mind my own business or I'd get the same treatment, but seeing that I was on my way, she simply walked off, muttering under her breath.

"Lie still," I called to Maria. "I'll bring you your rations and some coffee. Try to relax now."

She nodded gratefully as I left her flat on her back on the mat. When I returned with her ration of bread she whispered, "I just want something to drink. Please, bring me a little water."

"I can't bring you water, Maria." I tried to make her understand. "They're blowing the *Blocksperre* whistle—the guard won't let me out. Don't you hear it?"

The whistle signaled that no one could leave the barrack for any reason whatsoever. As the *stubowas* busily set up the buckets that served as toilets, they screamed at the insubordinate women trying to go out, "*Blocksperre! Strenge Blocksperre!* No one leaves!"

"But I'm so thirsty, I can't stand it," Maria groaned. "Bring me a drop of water. Sell my bread, just get me something to drink."

One would have thought, hearing such wailing and pleading, that we were lost in some vast desert, alone and perishing of thirst. In fact, we were only two miserable *Arbeitstücke* in Barrack 15 of Birkenau extermination camp, lost among hundreds, thousands like ourselves. And yet it was more desolate and inhuman here than in any barren desert.

"Take the bread and sell it," Maria pleaded. "Just bring me something to drink."

I took her ration of bread and went stalking up and down the aisles of the barrack, poking my head into every nook to ask if anyone could sell me a drop of coffee for a sick friend. But I was out of luck: the few poor souls who would have made the trade spread out their arms in a futile gesture — they had already drained their cups. So I wandered around, offering the bread in vain. Up above, in the cozy nooks on the balconies, I could see the *stubowas* cheerily eating their supper, but who would ever dare appeal to them? When they finished eating, they would wash their hands with the leftover coffee as usual. Nonetheless it was hopeless to ask; the chasm between our worlds was too great, and too daunting.

One of them spied me down below and stuck out her angry, red, balloon-shaped face. "What do you want? What are you looking for?"

"A little coffee for a sick woman, *Frau stubowa*. I'll sell you some bread if you want." But the gray bread that tasted like sawdust could hardly tempt these ladies accustomed to very different fare.

"Coffee? All gone," she replied, while the girl next to her raised a large flask to her lips. "It's gone, I'm telling you. Now would you just get away?"

I went back to our mat to find Maria really in a bad way, groaning and complaining so incessantly that the women nearby shouted at her to keep still and stop bothering them.

She tried her best to be quiet, but every few minutes she would cry out sharply. In between, she whispered, "Give me something to drink. Please, I beg you."

Again I set out with the bread and the bowl, in search of a drop of coffee. It was the last night of the holiday, though, so the women were gathered at the far end of the barrack opposite the room with the sinks, where the improvised Menorah, all eight candles lit, stood glittering on the white tablecloth.

Everyone was there, even Erna and the *stubowas*, praying and gazing at the candles with eyes aglow. I didn't even try to get near. I hadn't the heart to go back to Maria either, so I simply trailed up and down the aisles with the bread in my hand, listening to the murmured prayers and Maria's moaning.

"Water," she pleaded. "A drink of water."

"Grant us salvation, mercy, and solace," the others implored. Poised between them, I was overcome with mounting anguish.

I had passed by Adela's nook several times, but though I knew she wouldn't be at the services, I was so used to pre-tending she didn't exist that it hadn't occurred to me to try her. It was she who called out and, to my great wonder, spoke kindly, with concern.

"It's starting, eh?"

I didn't understand what was supposed to be starting.

"It's starting," she repeated. "At this rate she could give birth tonight."

Up to that moment I hadn't had the presence of mind to put two and two together. But of course Adela must be right, I realized. The pains were clearly growing more intense, heralding Erika's arrival. Moreover, since Maria was past her seventh month, in all likelihood the baby would be born alive. What would happen then? But the demands of the moment were pressing enough. I couldn't worry now about what was ahead for the infant.

"Give me a little coffee, will you?" I asked. "I'll trade you some bread for it."

"Wait just a minute." The old woman rummaged hastily around in her bunk and came up with her bowl, still full.

"I knew it," she cried, very pleased with herself. "I knew this was it—good thing I saved it. I could tell from her first groan."

She bustled about, full of good cheer, her eyes glittering not with the usual malice but a fond excitement.

"I'm going over there now," she informed me. "You don't know how to handle this, you're just a girl. I know about these things."

With that she took the bowl and hurried off to our bunk while I followed along, not knowing what to make of this stunning and rather dubious transformation. Could it be trusted? Or would that frenzied mind only cause more trouble? To all appearances Adela had crossed over from hate to love, but how long could it last?

"It'll be born on the last night of the holidays. That's good luck," she was saying. "Oh, just relax, take it easy. I know what has to be done."

A cluster of onlookers had gathered around Maria to watch in amazement, but when Adela arrived with the coffee, she ignored them. Grown expansive with energy, she bent over the suffering woman.

"Here, drink this and feel better, child," she said tenderly. "You'll see, it'll all go just fine."

Maria looked up at her, flabbergasted, then leaned toward the bowl Adela held out and drank in great thirsty gulps.

"Thank you," she whispered.

"No need to thank me, my dear child," the old woman cried. "I'm here now, I'll take care of everything, you'll see."

She turned on the inquisitive bystanders who were ready to find amusement in anything out of the ordinary. What were those rowdy loafers standing around gaping at? Who needs their nosy looks? What we could use are some nimble hands. Get back, let her have some air. The women scoffed and snickered, but Adela's face was so stern that they soon dispersed. Maria tossed fitfully while Adela hovered over her, fussing about to no purpose. She kept up a running patter and at one point turned and ordered me to get the bottles ready.

"Bottles? What bottles?"

She explained impatiently that it wouldn't be long now: we had to be prepared with boiling water, linens, towels. How ignorant could I be? As Maria's pains continued, the madwoman straightened the straw mat, emptied and wiped the bowl, and set out imaginary linens, all the while muttering bits of advice and pet-names jumbled together with memories of her youth.

The Block had grown silent. Only Maria and Adela were up, one mad, the other moaning. I was curled up in my corner, exhaustion having defeated human sympathy. Our morning would begin in the black of night.

I don't know how much later I was roused by Maria's shriek, but it couldn't have been long before reveille. I jolted up in fright: the young woman was writhing in pain, sweat pouring down her contorted face. Her hands groped along the mat for something to hang on to, until finally she clutched desperately at Adela's shoulders.

"It's coming," murmured Adela, rapt with joy. "Oh, my daughter, it's coming!"

The baleful crescendo had awakened the other women too, and word raced through the barrack that Maria was about to give birth. Everyone got up, from Erna and the *stubowas* to young girls with eyes glazed by sleep, and gathered around our bunk.

It was dark—the lights didn't go on until reveille—but Erna had someone bring a candle, which she held up close. Maria's screams became more and more piercing. I didn't know what to do—the ghastly shrieking sliced through me unbearably. I stroked her hand, icy, drenched with sweat. In the dim candlelight I could see Adela's ecstatic face and Erna's hard profile. In her beautiful red dressing-gown, Erna knelt on the straw, unmindful of the dirt.

The shimmering light played on Elenka's bony cheeks, Aërgi's red hair, Rosette's striped shirt. "*Oh, bonne Mère, bonne Mère!*" Rosette said over and over. "The baby is coming! Oh, listen to her yell, poor thing." And Erna, Elenka, Aërgi, Rosette, all the women assembled to witness the birth trembled with a quasi-mystical anticipation—the hushed, spiritual awe that attends the bloody rites of maternity.

"Just one more push," the old woman urged. "Ah, there you go, good girl, that's it!"

There was a last wildly piercing shriek, and suddenly, silence. Adela stood up holding something in her hands: a tiny, delicate red thing.

"The baby!" A murmur rippled through the crowd. "The baby!" Erna stepped forward to take the little red thing from Adela's hands, but she hung on to it fiercely. No one must touch the baby. No one! Even Erna was forced to yield: she simply picked up a rag and, with hands hardened by clenching into fists and wielding the club, she gently and lovingly wiped the newborn flesh.

I stared speechlessly at the infant, completely forgetting Maria. Then as I elbowed my way through to get a better view, I felt something wet and warm on my bare feet. I looked down. A stream of red dripped steadily, relentlessly from the mat and slowly spread over the bricks below.

"Maria!" I cried in panic. "Maria!" I grabbed the candle to look.

Maria neither spoke nor moaned any longer. She lay flat on her back, chalky white, while the stream flowed indefatigably, as though the source would never run dry.

"Maria, Maria!" I called. Suddenly the reveille gong sounded and the yellow lights flashed on. It was still night, but for us day was dawning, with its unvarying acts and imperatives, the harsh Birkenau day that acknowledged neither birth nor death, only silence and obedience to its pitiless laws.

After an instant of confusion the *stubowas* let out the usual morning cry, "*Aufstehen! Schnell, schnell, aufstehen!*" although everyone was already up and about. The women took off at a run; whoever wanted to use the toilets or splash their faces or gulp down some warm water had better hurry, run, push and shove: *schnell, schnell, schnell!* Only a few of us remained: Adela, holding the baby on her lap wrapped in a blanket, Erna, a couple of others, and I. We didn't speak, just looked back and forth from the infant's red head, half hidden by the blanket, to the blood dripping inexhaustibly from the mat.

"Maria?" I called softly. "Maria?"

The *Lagerkapo*'s shrill whistle blared from close by, and a terrified *stubowa* came running to find Erna: the *Lagerführer* was making the rounds, the women weren't even ready for roll-call. Had she lost her mind? She'd better get a move on, she could take care of all this later. The auxiliaries were on their way, the *Lagerführer* was practically here. Hurry up!

Erna jerked into action. Pouncing on Adela, she snatched away the infant and placed him next to his mother in the darkest corner of the bunk, then piled on blankets every which way to hide them both.

"The blood! Quick, wipe up the blood!" cried the *stubowa*.

I rushed over to Maria and raised the blanket. I thought I could hear her breathe.

"Don't worry, just lie still," I pleaded. "After roll-call they'll take you to the nurse. You'll be all right, you'll see."

Adela had refused to move, and the *stubowa* fell on her and beat her with satisfaction. At last there was someone to take it all out on: the lost sleep, the distressing night, the troubles that might still be in store. The old woman whimpered and tried to resist, but she was overpowered. I took her by the arm and dragged her outside like a sack of potatoes.

Everyone was already lined up for roll-call. I barely managed to slip into one of the last groups, pulling Adela along, when our auxiliary rounded the corner of the barrack, accompanied by the *Lagerführer*. Erna went to meet them.

The auxiliary had only recently arrived, and no doubt the *Lagerführer* had his eye on her. She was young and quite striking—tall, blond, with a rosy complexion—the most beautiful German in the camp, and she didn't even look especially ill-natured. He, on the other hand, was a lean, somber middle-aged man with a cruel, impassive face. It was obvious the girl couldn't find him very attractive, since she seemed to respond more out of duty than enthusiasm.

This morning, as always, they walked side by side, chatting. The blond girl proceeded up and down the rows with her pink forefinger raised, counting the "pieces" and jotting things down in her notebook.

"There's one missing," she observed.

"*Jawohl, Frau Aufseherin,*" replied Erna with a smile. "That one is inside, *kaputt*. As soon as roll-call is over I'll send for a stretcher."

And she moved toward the door, inviting the auxiliary to enter, for it was customary, on these rare and solemn occasions, for the German officer in charge to go into the barrack for verification.

I thought of the frail infant hidden under the blankets. Was he dead? Alive? I turned to Adela: her legs had buckled under her and she was sitting down, staring off into space as though in a trance.

"Are you out of your mind, sitting during inspection?" I hissed. "You want to have us all begging for mercy? You'll be the death of us!"

I pulled her roughly to her feet just in time to get back to attention myself. The German was coming out of the barrack and appeared calm, so it must have gone smoothly.

"All finished?" asked the *Lagerführer*, smiling and edging closer to her.

They left. When I released my savage grip on Adela's hand, she fell back down in a heap with her handkerchief covering her face, rather than the matted gray clumps of hair the *stubowa* had pulled with such delight. She held a trembling hand over her eyes, the same hand that had twitched all through roll-call. I waited on pins and needles for the whistle to free us, and when at last it blew, I yelled at Adela to hurry up, if we ran fast we could get back inside and see what was happening. But the old woman didn't move or answer. I couldn't waste any more time on her and ran toward the barrack. At the door I bumped into a *stubowa*.

"What's happening?" I asked anxiously. "How are they?" And the *stubowa* said, "All finished."

High Tension

The moment I flung open the door of Pressroom 16 the women darted away from the radiator, and Bruna tried to conceal something under her apron.

I had to laugh. I was in good spirits because I had finally gotten my job switched, a major improvement. For months on end I had been working in Kommandos filled with foreigners and feeling lost, surrounded and outnumbered by hostile strangers calling me "macaroni." It was a pleasure to be back with my own people for a while, where I could speak fast and freely, without struggling over tricky turns of phrase or seeking interpreters.

The others were glad too, and the exuberant Costanza came over to hug me. They advised me to hurry and find a place at one of the machines. We'd sit together and talk, and the time would pass more easily. I quickly stationed myself at the levers of the press and leaned over Bruna, sitting beside me, to see what she had rushed to hide when I startled them at the door.

"That looks pretty!" I exclaimed, peering down. "Did you make it yourself?"

Bruna smiled with pleasure and handed me her work so I could admire it more closely.

It was a pathetic little gray cardboard box, the corners stitched together by hand, lined with waxed paper, the kind they use in delicatessens. But what gave the thing a touch of class was the pencil drawing on the lid—two little stream-

ers, a heart, and the name "Pinin" written with fine flour-
ishes. Needless to say, in ordinary life any nursery-school
toddler would have scorned such an object, but in the lager
everything was different: that box could be worth half a slice
of bread.

"It's really lovely," I repeated with conviction. "I should
make one for myself. Every Sunday I hold my margarine in
my hand all through roll-call and half of it melts away. Is it
hard to find cardboard?"

"No," said Bruna, and she promised to make one for me
too, if I could locate the materials. Just then the door opened
and the German worker rushed in.

She was a frail, waxy-faced blond with a petulant face,
draped up to the chin in a patched-together scarf. Costanza,
with a kind of friendly sympathy typical of her Roman
nature, referred to her as "the Victim," the perfect nickname
for this morose figure.

But when the young worker faced us, her cold gray eyes
haughtily rebuffed any humane overtures; her voice held
nothing but reproach.

"Not in your places yet? Not even started? Come on, get
going! It's past six o'clock!"

So we took our places. The motors began humming, the
carriages rolling, the pressure gauges bouncing, and the
harshly lit little room pulsed with the throbbing of
machinery.

The women had warned me that chattering made the
German irritable, so I worked silently, yielding, as always,
to the familiar yet weird sensation that my arms were no
longer part of me. They moved back and forth of their own
accord, while my real self wandered far away: there was absolutely no connection between them.

The German had set to work too, inspecting the boxes, her hands moving briskly and efficiently, as though the entire outcome of the war depended on the amount of work Press 16 could turn out by the end of the day.

I was getting bored and felt like talking. It wasn't forbidden, after all, as long as you didn't abuse the privilege. Anyway, what harm in trying?

"What does your Pinin look like?" I asked Bruna. "I've never seen him. I was working the other shift. Is he a big boy?"

Bruna said he was thirteen, in fact his birthday was in a few days. He looked younger, though, because he was in such awful shape. When they got back, she would take him to the mountains for a few months. He was used to visiting his grandparents there and felt at home.

"We see each other every day on the way back from work," said Bruna, her face lighting up. "He goes out with a Kommando of boys to unload the garbage. It's just for a minute, but the Kapo isn't so bad, and Pinin can jump off the cart and run over to give me a hug. Hermine sees, but she pretends not to."

"That Hermine is okay," I broke in eagerly. "When I asked to switch groups, she let me do it right away. Not like that Kapo in Kommando 110, who slaps you around before you even open your mouth."

I wanted to tell Bruna the story of Mia and Lili Marlene from Kommando 110, but the Victim had already waved at us impatiently a few times and now she was glaring at me, so I had no choice but to turn back to the levers. Once more my arms went diligently about their business while my mind wandered far away.

The morning hours crept by one after the other, the color

of the windowpanes gradually growing lighter, until the bell rang and we were let out to have our soup. It was the same each day: the warmth of the turnips and the very brief interruption made us lethargic; we would suddenly be overcome by fatigue and dread: six hours passed, six more to go. Our heads drooped to the table, our bodies pleaded for rest; when the bell signaled the end of the break, we dragged ourselves to our feet and staggered back to work like drunkards.

And again the motors hummed, the carriages rolled, the machines throbbed. The windowpanes gradually darkened, and the Germans changed shifts. The strokes of the levers were sluggish now, and no one felt like talking. As I watched young Mirella's eyes sink into dark rings, her arms moving more wearily with every stroke, I thought gloomily of when we had first met. Who would ever recognize us now?

In a corner of the room hung a large round white clock, but we couldn't hear it ticking. Costanza went over to check the time every other minute.

"Three-quarters of an hour to go. Forty-five minutes. Forty. Dammit!" she grumbled in exasperation. "This last hour will never end. Never!"

But even that last eternal hour finally came to an end, and at the sound of the bell, we burst through the door like children released from school. Outside, the elderly *Posten* waited to escort us back, first counting us over and over like the old cranks that they were. At last the Kommando was in order and Hermine started marking time in military fashion.

"*Links, links, links, und links.* Left, left . . ."

The factory was a short distance beyond Auschwitz. We had several kilometers to go before reaching Birkenau, and once we had passed the railroad bridge, the road stretched out in a straight line through the faded, dingy country-side.

Night was falling. The first star glimmered in the serene twilight sky, the splendidly bright star Costanza called her own and watched tenderly, as if awaiting precious portents. The shadows softly settling on the earth promised rest and oblivion. We had gotten through another day. But what would the next one bring? I was walking along immersed in this mingled sense of anxiety and melancholy, when I felt someone tug at my arm. Bruna was pointing out a certain place in the road.

"It was right there that I saw him two months ago," she told me. "I remember as if it was yesterday. I had just started in the factory, and I saw a cart coming by with a group of boys pulling it. My heart gave a leap. I just had this feeling Pinin must be there. Hermine was alongside of me, and when she saw me get out of line she started screaming, you know how she does, '*Verrückt, verrückt!* Are you crazy!' and she pushed me back. I don't know how to explain it. I just pointed to the truck and said, 'My baby! Right over there! My baby!' 'Ba-by?' Hermine said. '*Was ist* ba-by? *Was ist das?* Oh, you're out of your mind.' The cart was closer now, and there was Pinin pulling the shaft. *Madonna mia*, what they did to him! I tell you, if I weren't his own mother I wouldn't have known him. I hollered out, 'Pinin, Pinin!' and he stared as if he thought he was dreaming. Finally he saw me. He leaped from the cart and threw himself on my neck, so tight that wild horses couldn't have pulled him off. . . ."

She stopped to wipe her eyes and so did Costanza, walking on her other side. I squeezed Bruna's arm affectionately.

"And then what? Tell me, I like hearing it. . . ."

So Bruna told the whole story: how they were arrested, how clever Pinin had been when they interrogated him. He didn't panic but answered exactly as she and his father had instructed him. Bruna had been living in Milan then. Her house was bombed. She was sure she would never find any of the things she had managed to save. But what do things matter? You can always get new ones if you work. The important thing was to get home. As for the house and all, she never gave it a thought.

We were going along chatting contentedly when I noticed one of those big gray garbage carts approaching down a side street, exactly as Bruna had described it. I was suddenly eager to see Pinin.

"Where is he?" I asked.

But Bruna wasn't paying attention. She was changing places with the woman ahead of her in line, then with the next and the next, till she had moved up right opposite the cart.

A small boy broke away from the long shafts to come running toward our lines. I couldn't get a good look because the others were leaning out too, so as not to miss this scene, but I did catch a glimpse of a pale, emaciated fair-haired boy all wrapped up in a black jacket, wearing the striped lager cap.

"Get back here!" shouted the boys' Kapo. "Get back, Italian!"

But the child clung to his mother's embrace. He was telling her something, looking quite disconsolate, while Bruna kept shaking her head, no, no. Meanwhile she adjusted the cap on his shaved head, straightened out his jacket, and kissed him.

"They're breaking my heart," muttered Costanza, beside me. "They do it every time, and I don't even have a hanky anymore. Those pigs took that away too."

She blew her nose noisily and I did too, as we watched Hermine trying to chase the boy away, yelling that this was a lager and they would end up smothering each other with their kisses. But Pinin wouldn't let go. He dug in his heels and hung on tight, until Bruna herself had to push him away before the Kapos lost their tempers.

So Pinin returned to the cart and Bruna got back in line as the squad resumed its brisk pace in time to Hermine's military *links und links*.

"So long, Pinin," I called as we passed the cart.

When he raised his head I could see how small and worn out he was. He tugged at the strap of the cart, digging in his heels like one of those wretched abused little donkeys you sometimes see along the country roads.

"Home soon!" I called out—the lager's constant motto. He nodded yes, home soon, then bent his body to one side, seeking the least painful way to keep going. That was the last I saw of him.

Bruna didn't sleep in my bunk, and much as I wanted to know what Pinin had said, it didn't cross my mind to go looking for her—I was so desperate to lie down. After roll-call I rushed straight to my straw mat. The other women might line up for coffee or go off to steal peelings from the compost heap, but I was always the first to get to my niche: nothing could flavor my bread so well as those few moments of silence and solitude.

I was stretched out, thinking of nothing at all, just leisurely chewing and rechewing each bite, when Bruna came by, carrying her ration.

"Come to the market with me," she begged. "I want to get something for Pinin. You know a little German, come on."

It was such a comfort to lie still, I hadn't the least desire to move. But Bruna was so set on going that I didn't have the heart to refuse. I'd simply have to make the best of it.

"Okay, but let's be quick about it," I groaned. "I can't desert my bed. Just yesterday one of my blankets was 'organized.'"

Bruna promised we'd be done in no time, and we hurried out behind the "Redheads'" barrack, the camp's official black market and trading post.

Along the way, she told me Pinin wasn't feeling well. He found the work more strenuous every day, and he'd burst into tears, recounting how one of the boys had taunted, "Hey you, Italian! Macaroni to the crematorium, get going!"

Bruna tightened her lips as she repeated this, and her eyes glistened. To change the subject, I asked what she was planning to buy. For half a ration of bread she could get a quarter of a cabbage or two potatoes, although the most practical thing was carrots. They contained lots of vitamins: three carrots are better than a steak, did she know that? Seriously, I had read it the last time I saw a newspaper.

At the market, we started looking around for some good bargains. Unfortunately, it was late by this time and only a few women still hung around listlessly. We were offered two cigarettes, a piece of lard, and even some little green apples, but these were luxury items, not suitable for us. What really appealed to us was a gorgeous half of a cabbage.

"Ask the lowest price," said Bruna, entranced.

But the rock-bottom price was a ration and a half of bread, so we had to go away disappointed.

Bruna was getting worried. There were carrots for sale every single night. How come just tonight we couldn't find any?

"We'll find them," I assured her. "I know who must have some. Katia from Kommando 9. She'll give us a good price, too."

Katia was a Russian I had met back when I worked with poor Zinuchka. She had a swarthy round face and could be tough and suspicious, but she remembered me and smiled.

"You want carrots? Sure, I got hold of three. Big, fresh, top quality, my carrots."

She unrolled the rag she was holding to display three lovely copper-colored carrots. There was a little onion, too. Katia wanted to make a package deal: carrots and onion for a ration and a half of bread.

I protested that my friend couldn't afford that. We weren't interested in the onion. A half ration of bread was more than enough for the three carrots. Was it a deal?

No, no deal. Katia had risked the *Strafkommando* (Punishment Kommando) to get that stuff. She was hungry too, she couldn't give things away. It was no use. Forget it.

As was customary during these heated negotiations, several curious bystanders had gathered round to take part in the discussion, assessing the carrots and the ration of bread, debating the relative merits of the offers and the quality of the merchandise.

"Tell her it's for my son," Bruna urged.

"What does she care?" I answered brusquely.

It struck me as futile to introduce that sort of issue. I knew that at Birkenau a slice of black bread was practically worthless, and besides, what earthly difference could it make to Katia if Bruna's son needed carrots? So did everyone else. She certainly hadn't risked the *Strafkommando* in order to feed Pinin.

"Tell her I'll give her the whole ration," insisted Bruna, determined at this point not to leave empty-handed.

"And what'll you eat?" I retorted. "Can you live on air? Do you want to go to the crematorium before Pinin?"

Bruna replied angrily that this was no concern of mine—I should stick to being the interpreter. I was offended in turn and translated her offer word for word to Katia, who, after some lengthy wavering, decided to accept, and the deal was concluded. We were about to leave when Katia called us back. I was afraid she had changed her mind and would demand to have her carrots, but to our great astonishment she handed me a minuscule slice of onion, saying we should give it to the boy. Then she dashed off, leaving us gazing dumbfounded at this incredible gift.

"If only the Greek doesn't steal it!" said Bruna anxiously. "It's so awful to sleep with a thief. You can't ever relax. Just last night she nibbled up a piece of bread someone had left over for the morning. A regular rat! Look, why don't you take this stuff and hang on to it till tomorrow, otherwise I'll be up all night guarding it."

So I wrapped the carrots and the onion in my handkerchief and put it in my bowl, which also served as a pillow, never imagining what an ordeal I had in store.

Once I got to bed, it was as if a noxious fluid oozed through the aluminum, not letting me sleep. The golden carrots and tangy onion danced behind my closed eyes, and several times I ran my fingers lightly over the bowl with a violent urge to pick it up. I didn't want to steal poor Pinin's food, only to smell it, to savor the wonderful fresh, raw smell. I hadn't smelled anything like it since I was arrested.

It was all I could do to control myself, and in the end, blessed sleep came to my rescue. I dreamed I was with Bruna and Pinin in a huge field of cabbages. I plucked a leaf and put it in my mouth, and it turned into a soft, sweet, fragrant slice of *panettone*. I could taste the sweetness of the cake melting in my mouth. Pinin was laughing because it was a holiday and the bells were ringing. . . .

It wasn't bells, but the harsh gong of Birkenau sounding reveille. I opened my eyes and immediately closed them. The punishment of the day ahead weighed mercilessly on my mind, still numb from sleep. Why did the night fly by so fast? Why couldn't it go on forever? Why couldn't a merciful God turn all the rest of the war into one prolonged night?

My eyes were still closed when Bruna came to get her things. "What's your hurry?" I asked, seeing her all ready. "Did you fall out of bed or are you on kitchen duty?"

She explained that she had gotten up before reveille to do chores for a *stubowa* who was too genteel to fetch buckets of water. So Bruna would do it; in return the *stubowa* had promised her a few potatoes.

"You're crazy," I scolded, truly indignant. "You didn't eat last night, and today you get up early to carry buckets of water. You look like a wreck. Is this doing your son any good?"

But of course Bruna replied that carrying two buckets of

water was a joke. She had carried lots more in her time, even as a child. Why, at Pinin's age she was already working in the rice fields, then in the foundry, and after that in a factory. With all those younger brothers and sisters at home, she was no stranger to hunger and work. No, what really worried her was the new shifts starting on Monday: the night schedule for next week would make it impossible to see Pinin. Seven days without any news, without being able to do anything for him — now *that* would be hard!

Bruna carried around the precious package all day, and in the evening, when the garbage cart passed by and Pinin made his usual dash over to our lines, we all watched her surprise him with the treat.

"I'll bring you more next Monday," she cried. "Don't worry. Good-bye till Monday."

We all cried, "Good-bye, Pinin, good-bye," as we passed. His mouth was already full, but he waved gaily.

I remembered, then, that Bruna had said Monday was his birthday. A birthday in the lager, poor Pinin! What could we do to brighten it up a bit?

I had had my birthday in the lager too, and I recalled how depressed I was, and then how deeply touched and comforted when my friend Cucciolo from Fiume, elegant and freckle-faced, presented me with a small slice of salted bread and a tiny curl of margarine. Even in the lager, she tried to do things with style. I decided to emulate her and asked the others if they would put aside a morsel of bread each day. That way, within a week we could have enough saved up to buy something for Pinin.

They agreed readily — we'd be just as hungry either way — and by the end of the week we triumphantly purchased half a clove of garlic and handed it solemnly over to Bruna, to add to the other items she had scraped together by skipping meals and hauling buckets.

She was very moved. Her sallow face colored with surprise as she thanked us, and with her black eyes glistening under the thick brows, she even seemed beautiful. She had the noble, slightly haughty look of a creature who was worn down, yes, but not brutalized, whose spirit was kept intact, not yet governed by vileness and fear. And that, amidst the hard, brutal faces of Birkenau, was a wonder to behold.

Monday rolled round at last. For seven days now we hadn't glimpsed a patch of bright sky: we marched to work in the dark and marched back in the dark. Even our faint memories of the sun were slipping away. Night after night, with eyes bloodshot from the bare bulbs, we dreamed of radiant blue skies.

But the new week brought no change. The world was shrouded in an eerie fog, and the smoke from the crematorium hung low and stagnant in the heavy air. Winter was on the way—rain, icy wind and snow, selections and frozen feet—the merciless Birkenau winter that crowded its victims into death's waiting room, for there was far too much work and the six crematoria just couldn't keep up.

We marched with our heads bowed in the pre-dawn darkness, and even Hermine's voice sounded apathetic. Much as we detested the work, we couldn't wait to get to the pressroom, beyond the realm of cold and rain. As we passed other squads on their way to work in the fields, their eyes flashed an almost venomous message of envy, an envy we knew well enough from our early days.

The minute we got inside we huddled around the radiator

and our clothes began to smoke. We were hoping to dry off, but the German rushed in frowning and ordered us to get started, then sat down with her head bent.

"Look, she's in mourning," whispered Costanza.

Indeed, there was a black ribbon on the young woman's dress. But no outward sign was needed: the grief showed plainly in her washed-out face, her distraught eyes.

"Poor thing," said Costanza, forgetting for the moment, in typical Italian fashion, to wish death and eternal damnation at least ten times a day to every German on earth. "Poor thing. Her life is no bed of roses either. She must have lost someone in an air raid."

Perhaps sensing her sympathy, the Victim glanced up to find Costanza looking at her as if to extend some sisterly understanding. But the German wrinkled her brow and reprimanded her sternly. "Work, work, get a move on! What are you stopping for? *Das ist Sabotage!*"

"Goddammit!" Costanza muttered. "What the hell are these people made of anyway?"

We learned later, from what the German told the one taking the next shift, that her family had been killed in a bombing. She also hadn't had news of her husband in ages. How much worse could it get? But by now we had gotten past pitying her. We could regard her wasted face with indifference and a grim impulse of revenge. "Let her see what it feels like," someone remarked. And we recognized, too, that words such as expiation, suffering, punishment were utterly beside the point. No one can atone for another's grief; all the combined suffering of the Germans could never make up for our own, not for a single quarter of an hour in the shadow of the crematorium, our teeth chattering in the cold, our eyes fixed on the curls of smoke drifting overhead.

It rained steadily, and we worried that Pinin's cart might return early and we wouldn't get to give him our presents. At last the day was over, and we emerged into a light mist, with veils of fog condensing on the gray countryside.

"There they are, they're coming!" Costanza suddenly shouted. Peering through the fog, we could just make out the boys' cart creeping laboriously along the soggy road. We were overjoyed and craned our necks to find Pinin and wish him happy birthday.

"He's not there," cried Bruna, who had moved ahead in the line. "Pinin isn't there! Look!"

Her face was transformed. The rest of us, caught up in her hysteria, began screaming for him at the top of our lungs as the boys watched impassively, not even responding. Finally a Greek boy with deep black sullen eyes called out, "The Italian? He's gone. He went to the rest Block."

"Rest Block?" The blood rushed to Bruna's face. "Did you say rest Block? He's not working?"

The boy shook his head and turned away, adding casually that Pinin was still in the quarantine lager. Maybe we'd see him as we passed. And we did indeed: he was behind the mesh of high tension wires that surrounded the camp, those wires unmarked by any warning skull and crossbones. The entire camp was devoted to death. How absurd it would be to warn people against the lady of the house.

Pinin wasn't alone. There was a tiny snot-nosed kid of five or six years old hanging on his arm, pale as a cadaver, swallowed up in his striped coat. When Pinin caught sight of us, he shouted something and started to run, but one of the *Posten* in the wooden turrets leaned out, pointing his gun and bellowing. So we had to move on, and Bruna couldn't get near him even for a moment.

Her fair-haired son stood there desolate, watching us leave. Then he walked on beside the ditch as if to follow us, dragging along the little one, who kept sliding around in the muck. They were so small and alone in their misery that I didn't have the heart to look. I turned around and kept walking, my eyes straight ahead.

None of us could bear to look at Bruna either, right beside us, though every so often we exchanged meaningful glances behind her back. We all felt the awkward strain of needing to speak, to say something to this grief-stricken mother. Ah, poor Bruna! Why did she have to find Pinin only to lose him like this? Better not to have seen him at all. At least she might have kept a shred of hope.

Had she been a newcomer, we might have tried to persuade her that the rest Block was a good place to be, a place where you got your strength back. But Bruna had come to the camp before us and no merciful deception was possible: she knew what the verdict was. She knew that for a day or two or three, maybe even a week, Pinin would rest in the barrack, until one night the selections truck would carry him off to rest in heaven.

And what were we supposed to do? Deny the facts? Cry out to God? Curse mankind? It was all futile now, all too late—Pinin was already there.

I couldn't help thinking, as I marched, about his birthday and the hard-won gift. Poor Bruna, we murmured like a litany, poor Bruna, poor Pinin! What else was there to say? Even later on, when Bruna disappeared and we could speak freely, all our thoughts and feelings seemed to add up to nothing but that simple, stupid phrase: poor Bruna, poor Pinin.

After a while Costanza went to look for Bruna and found

her stretched out on her mat with her head buried in her arms. She had tried to speak to her, she said, but Bruna wanted to be left alone and so she went away. What else could she do? It was better, in the long run, to let her give in to her feelings. Once the first shock had worn off, we'd keep her company and try to comfort her.

So naturally we went off to sleep. Although I could summon the best will in the world to get to sleep, it always took forever. Every fiber of my being craved sleep, yet that same fitful exhaustion kept me wide awake and restless. I couldn't stop seeing Bruna's face when the boy said rest Block: crimson, turgid with blood, deranged. And the rain, and the two boys behind the electrified fence—Pinin with those dazed, terrified eyes, and the ghostly little one clinging to his arm and slipping around in the muck. I pictured Bruna lying awake in despair, and it struck me how craven we had been. It wasn't for her sake that we'd left her alone, but because we couldn't bear to get too close to her anguish.

Suddenly I had a tremendous urge to see her and talk to her. I tiptoed past the sleeping bodies and down the passageway to the end, the dank nook where Bruna slept. She was sitting on the floor, motionless in the shadows, her shoulders hunched in the corner and her head in her hands.

"Why aren't you in bed?" I whispered.

"I can't stay still," she said. "It disturbs the others, so I got up. I'm better off here. . . ."

I got down next to her and put my arm around her, and we sat that way for a while, not speaking. Then she started to cry. She cried soundlessly, stifled little sobs, out of regard for the others who were asleep. Her hot tears rained down on my hands.

"Why?" she whispered every few minutes. "Why, Liana, why?"

I had no answer to this desolate question. I could only hold her close, sighing and echoing, "Yes, why? Why does life have to be so hard and death so painful? Any God who could think this up for his amusement must be very cruel."

We sat there for quite a while, now and then whispering a few words, till my eyelids drooped with exhaustion; I needed to sleep. Bruna was weeping silently and I felt I shouldn't abandon her, but I was exhausted and had to work the next day. Feeling slightly ashamed of myself, I whispered that I would try to get some rest, it was late. She refused to go back to bed, so I left her sitting up alone.

The next day, Bruna took her seat in the pressroom and got to work. During roll-call, too, she had kept her distance: her face was a sullen chalky mask, and when we tried to show some affection or concern, she responded with irritation or not at all. So we let her be, except for some furtive glances.

"Let's hope she doesn't flip out," Costanza whispered. "Look at those eyes, will you? She doesn't even know what she's doing."

I shrugged and set to work. Life in Birkenau was so impossible that anyone could go crazy. People got used to it— Bruna would have to do likewise. The German's family was *kaputt* also, and yet if not for that black ribbon, no one would have noticed a thing. She'd gotten meaner, that's all, which was only natural. Everyone got mean—what else can people do when they feel totally crushed and hopeless?

I was absorbed in this train of thought, absent-mindedly doing my work, when I heard Costanza announce that the machine was out of order. She had figured out a way to cause these minor breakdowns, simply to have a few minutes' rest, and even though I liked the idea myself, I worried that she was starting to overdo it. The Victim had already threatened to report us to the *Meister* (civilian foreman), a burly, irascible red-faced man whose green Tyrolean hat with the little feather sticking straight up had earned him the nickname of "Bristly."

"*Maschine kaputt?*" the German inquired, looking up.

"*Maschine kaputt!*" replied Costanza with enthusiasm.

Her voice was too gleeful for the German not to notice. She got up, sweeping us with her icy glance, and left the room without a word, at which point we promptly gathered around the radiator to warm our hands. Bruna kept right on working. We tried to cajole her into joining us, but she was stubbornly impenetrable.

"Leave me alone," she shot back. "Just let me be, it's better that way. What can you do?"

We could do nothing, alas, so we returned to the radiator, holding out our hands and leaning down to let our faces bask in the gentle, lukewarm caress.

"Let's hope the mechanics are busy," said Costanza. "They make me so mad, the way they're always jeering at us."

Just then the door opened. We barely managed to get away from the radiator in time as the Victim entered, followed by the *Meister*. She must have given her report already, because the man began raging thunderously, lightning bolts erupting from his bloodshot little eyes. He ranted and raved, never pausing for breath, filling the pressroom with his guttural voice, while we stood taking it all in without comprehending a single word.

"Punishment!" he said finally, as clearly as possible. "You make sabotage this time, everyone *kaputt*, understand?"

We exchanged stealthy looks: this was coming to a bad end. We were slinking to the door in a hangdog way when Bruna, who up to that moment had shown no interest whatsoever in the scene, rose from her table to follow us.

"You, no!" said the *Meister*, signaling her to remain. "You work, you not like this gang of loafers. Good girl, you."

Bruna frowned in an effort to grasp the meaning of the words. And apparently she understood perfectly, for once again the blood rushed to her face. She eyed the German darkly, with a look of such evident outrage and loathing that he stared back in amazement and let out a filthy curse.

"Are you crazy?" he shrieked.

But Bruna kept her eyes riveted on him, radiating an infinite contempt. Then she deliberately spit at the huge man. Once, twice, and then she was down, his hob-nailed boots knocking her back and forth across the floor.

I tried in vain to explain she had lost her head because her child was *kaputt*; the boy was sent to the rest Block and she cracked under the strain.

"You should all be *kaputt*, that's what you deserve! We're too good to you!"

So I got my share too, and so did others who weren't even involved. Finally they flung us out into the yard on our hands and knees. It was a relief to feel the cool, misty air on our burning skin.

They left us there till evening, our blood pounding so hard that it was a while before we felt the damp seeping into our stiff bones. We were chilled and scared. They had threatened us with the *Strafkommando*, but what had we done wrong? None of us had spit, for heaven's sake! They would shave our heads again, we wouldn't have a minute's peace, and all for what? Would it save her son's life? We would be sent to the *Strafkommando* and he would die all the same, and that was that.

I looked at Costanza and could see the identical thoughts in her eyes. She too must feel rage and bitterness rising in her heart like a dark tide, flooding everything except fear of the unknown, fear of tomorrow, disgust, exhaustion. Over toward Birkenau, a few wisps of black smoke hung stagnant in the dense air. As I shifted around, trying to get the edge of my dress under my knees, which stung from the gravel, I felt a surge of anger. I was furious with myself and all the miserable creatures around me who prolonged their own suffering, eating themselves alive and leaving the Germans the final nuisance of setting them free.

Why not get it over with ourselves, set ourselves free? But no, we were too cowardly for that.

At last they called us. The other women were already lined up, and since the news of our misfortune had made the rounds, some nervy one went over to ask Bruna if it was true they had taken her number to send her to the rest Block.

She turned away in annoyance. Her bruised face remained impassive, even when the coarse Hermine pushed her roughly. Hermine wasn't bad-natured, but she didn't want trouble in her command, and Bruna, with her insane act, had violated that fixed principle. She was *verrückt*, out of her mind, how could she be forgiven?

We set out at a fast pace: it was about to rain, and the *Posten* wanted to reach the lager without getting soaked. No one said a word. With heads bowed, we brooded on the *Strafkommando*, on what might happen tomorrow, as the hard, enervating factory work took on the rosy nostalgic hues of a lost paradise.

It was drizzling: fog darkened the earth and sky. I marched, as I often did, with my eyes closed, timing the route, calculating the number of steps and making little bets with myself. All of a sudden I was crashing into the person in front of me. The lines were out of step. We were stopping. What was going on? I opened my eyes: we were opposite the *Quarantänelager*. I heard screaming and saw Bruna run toward the electrified fence. On the other side stood her son, gazing at her.

"Come to Mama!" cried Bruna, her arms outstretched. "Come to Mama, Pinin! Run!"

The boy hesitated for an instant. But his mother kept calling until he rushed to the fence, entreating her, "Mama, Mama!" As he hit the wires, his arms melted into his mother's in an explosion of violet flames. A buzzing sound zipped through the violently shaken wires, and the pungent smell of scorched flesh filled the air.

"What's going on, what's happening?" screamed the *Posten*, running over. "Goddamned gang of bitches, what is it now?"

But it was too late. They stood around yelling and cursing for a while, and then, realizing it was getting late and they had to be back at the lager for roll-call, they angrily ordered us to start marching.

"Quick, quick, move it!" they raged, as the rain poured down in buckets.

The line reassembled and Hermine began marking time. I turned for one last look: Bruna and Pinin lay in their tight embrace, the mother resting her head on the son's, as if to watch over his sleep.

The Five-Ruble Bill

Zina shook down her thermometer and declared, "Tomorrow I'm going back to work."

I rubbed mine vigorously against the blanket. "Well, not me."

"You mean you'd rather stay here and maybe get picked in a selection?"

"I'll risk a dozen selections," I snapped back stubbornly.

My bunkmate and I had the same spirited dialogue every day. She couldn't wait to leave despite her fever, while I, not at all feverish, longed to stay in *Himmelkommando* (Heaven Kommando): the danger of an impromptu selection struck me as entirely negligible compared to the rare bliss of lying on my mat undisturbed from morning to night.

"Anyway, you only want to leave so you can see your husband," I taunted her good-humoredly. The young woman smiled in assent, one of her many virtues being a serene acknowledgment of the truth.

"Tomorrow I'll pass the medical exam, and if I manage to get sent to Kommando 9, I'll see him the next day, won't I?"

"Yes, but what about your fever?"

"Oh, *Scheiss* fever!" Zinuchka grunted. "No one'll bother checking whether I have a fever or not. All that matters is that two days from now I'll see him!"

She was so excited at the prospect that she leaned over and hugged me. "Just two days till I see him, just two more days!" she sang out. Her eyes were so aglow with eagerness and love that I didn't have the heart to scold.

Even though Zina was sicker than I, she put up a good fight, struggling as best she could against the current, while I just let myself drift along. I could never quite make up my mind on the eternal question of whether to get passionately involved in life or simply give up and watch from the sidelines. Still, Zina was younger, and I felt it was my duty to talk sense to her again.

"You'll never be able to take the work." I touched her hands. "You feel very hot. What's your temperature?"

"Ninety-eight point six," Zina said slyly, showing me the thermometer.

I showed her mine. "Almost a hundred and two." We burst out laughing. Our tricks were very effective.

The thought of Grigori was what gave her the strength to resist, while my calm resignation came from depression. Which made more sense, under the circumstances? Who was right?

I had no idea, but that didn't stop me from trying to reason with her. Her plan was sheer folly, I said. After a month in bed and still walking around feverish, she would only destroy herself in that notorious Kommando 9, known throughout the camp as "Kommando 9 that works till nine." She had waited so long, surely she could wait a little longer, especially now that she knew her husband was in Birkenau. . . .

Zinuchka let me run on this way without saying a word, her sharp little face tilted in the pose of a schoolgirl dutifully attending to the lesson. Then, with a mischievous grin, she broke into the Russian tune she had taught me and knew I liked:

Johnny, you keep chasing me, but it's no use,
Johnny, you make eyes at me, but it's no use at all.

I was hurt. "You're making fun of me!" I cried.

"I'm not making fun of you. I'm singing."

Just then the nurse came by to check the thermometers, and she jotted something down in our folders. As an added precaution, I stretched out in a pose of sluggish lethargy, as befit the victim of mysterious and obstinately high temperatures. Zina bounced up in a display of energy.

"I'm feeling fine, nurse. Can I take the medical tomorrow?"

"Of course you'll take it. Why should you stay here if you have no fever? You think you're a lady of leisure?"

She left with Zina's chart, and I sat back up, delighted to have earned at least one more day of peace.

Zina wrapped herself in the blanket to step outside for a breath of air, as I lay alone brooding in the heavy August torpor. I'd be very sorry to see her go. God knows what sort of rude or nasty character might take her place, spoiling my comfortable set-up. On the other hand, she was so glad to be leaving. I closed my eyes and tried to envision her reunion with her husband, whom she had described as a good-looking fellow. I pictured him as one of those strapping young Russians I used to see passing by with a special Kommando. She'd find him changed, no doubt, but what difference would that make? She'd be overjoyed simply to see him.

I fell asleep. When I woke, Zina was back, carefully assembling her worldly possessions, the standard assets of a prosperous lager inmate: spoon, handkerchief, fragment of toothless comb, sliver of mirror. After wrapping and unwrapping the package several times, she unfolded, yet again, the crumpled bit of paper that had brought her the great news. The almost illegibly scrawled words—"Szafarisc is working in Kommando 9"—were more precious to her than all the riches on earth. Like any woman in love, she could pore over them endlessly with fond concentration, perusing every stroke of the handwriting, every detail of the paper, in an attempt to merge with the sender. For lack of anything better to do, I eavesdropped on the women in the next bunk.

"They're advancing every day," one was saying. "If they keep it up, the war'll be over by the end of the month."

"Yes, do you hear the artillery?" the other one seconded. "It must be aimed at Cracow. You'll see, any day now we'll wake up free."

I naturally pricked up my ears, but at the same time these absurd discussions always irritated me: if the Russians had actually been near Cracow, the camp would have been evacuated. Yet despite my annoyance I wished they would keep on jabbering—it was a thrill simply to hear the words: the war would be over by the end of the month, one day soon we'd wake up free.

Indeed, as if to confirm their optimism, the air raid siren blared and the Block erupted in enthusiasm. "*Fliegeralarm! Fliegeralarm!*" was the joyful cry from every corner. At once, the *Blocksperre* whistle pealed and the nurses rushed to close the doors, standing guard so that no one went out.

"They're shooting!" one woman called out excitedly.

"They're shooting, they're shooting!" ten more chimed in.

A series of hollow shots thudded in the distance like a garbled drumroll, then came a pause, and then a crackling of sharp, single shots. There were cries of, "Quiet, quiet, we can't hear," and in the stillness that followed came the unmistakable, the miraculous, deafening drone of engines flying over the camp and away.

A great tide of joy and hope swept over us. In that faraway August of 1944, every prisoner in Birkenau was certain that liberation couldn't be more than two weeks off. "If we can just hang on a little longer," we would tell each other. Our buoyant hum of gladness was pierced by the cries of the Frenchwoman who had been moaning for two nights straight.

"I don't want to die," she wailed. "I don't want to die just when the war is ending. I want to see my children."

It was a notably eventful day: no sooner had the air raid siren stopped than we heard the prolonged peal commonly known as *Fritzalarm*, which alerted the sentry posts to an escaped prisoner. At this signal the *Posten* (SS troops) would take off with their police dogs to hunt the man down, while the whole lager held its breath in panic, every heart beating as one with the bold fugitive at that very instant racing to freedom—or was it death?—his life hanging perilously in the balance.

The day, punctuated by alarms, was finally over. As darkness fell, the nurses turned out the lights, leaving only one in the center of the room, covered with a reddish paper shade. They ordered us to be quiet and went off to bed. For a time the Frenchwoman kept wailing that she didn't want to die now that the war was almost over. And then all was quite still.

The next day was Friday, the day of the medical exams, and I woke in a bad mood because Zina would be leaving.

"Good morning," I said, reaching out my hand. "How do you feel?"

"Fine," she replied curtly. I didn't want to upset her by suggesting otherwise, but she looked like she hadn't slept. She was paler than usual and had deep circles under her eyes. The nurses were shouting at people to get ready, Dr. Koenig was on his way, which always involved a tremendous flurry of activity. The patients were supposed to leave their shirts on the counter and line up to wait.

Zina climbed down from the bunk and joined the other women busily preparing to leave, each of them anxious and fretful about venturing once again into the unknown. Every aspect of life in the lager was ordered this way: the women were leaving behind the straw mats that had become familiar, uncertain where they would sleep that night, what part of the camp they might be sent to, what work they would be assigned or what companions would be working alongside them. They couldn't even be sure of staying alive, for a medical inspection might always have surprises in store, and Dr. Koenig wasn't keen on haggard faces, gray hair, and sagging bodies.

For those of us who remained, the medical exams offered a distraction, as well as the satisfaction of taking it easy while others sweated it out. Leaning back on our mats, we watched the spectacle with a certain condescension—a performance we knew by heart.

I didn't have a good view since my bunk was near the door, but when it was Zina's turn I did my best to see what would happen. Not a thing! Like all the rest, she filed past the doctor, who barely gave her a glance, simply waved her along with his pencil. She promptly grabbed her shirt and climbed happily back into the bunk.

"Did you see? I made it! I always manage to do whatever I set out to do."

"Because you're so stubborn." I had to smile at her pleasure. "Now put your shirt back on, or you'll be more *kaputt* than you already are."

She did as I said, then spent the rest of the day in silence, her face troubled. I assumed that as the moment of leaving the infirmary approached, she was getting anxious: countless worries until then kept at bay must be surging up.

"What's bothering you?" I asked. "You were so happy this morning."

"I am happy," she said, "but I'm also scared, you know."

"Scared? You passed the medical. What are you scared of now?"

"It's not that," Zina blurted out in frustration. "Don't you get it? I'm scared because I'm going to see him. It was January when I first got here. We stood in the snow all day long with our feet freezing, and the soup was even worse than it is now. They did everything they could think of to kill us, but I forced myself to keep going, just on the chance of seeing him again. I'm on my last legs, you can see for yourself, but I'm still willing to go and dig in Kommando 9. The only thing is, what if he's not there. . .?"

"But why wouldn't he be there? You got that note."

"Yes, sure, but let's just say for some reason he isn't there. Then I'd really be done for — just a bag of bones without the strength to stand on my feet. It wouldn't even be worth waiting for them to send me to the crematorium. I might as well go straight there myself."

"And if he is there?" I interrupted.

"If he is," she said, faltering, "well, then I think I just might die anyway. So there!"

She made me laugh. Here she was planning to die either way, I said, when every morning she scolded me for counting up how much longer I'd see the light of day—for I was convinced I would die at the first frost. Why not promise, instead, to come back and tell me all about her reunion with Grigori? She could sneak in early in the morning, before roll-call. Okay?

Zina solemnly promised to come, and later on when the nurses trooped in loudly to round up the women who were leaving, she promised again. We had tears in our eyes, but it would only be worse to have an emotional scene, so we said good-bye in haste and Zina left, wrapped in the gray blanket.

I had been in the infirmary once before, so I knew precisely what Zinuchka's day would be like. First the nurses would take her to the showers, and then there'd be the endless wait in the huge room where the ladies of the clerical staff sat puffed up with pride at tables overflowing with file cards. Since she spoke Slavic, Zina had a good chance of making herself heard, and yet in the long run, they really wouldn't be doing her much of a favor by sending her to the infamous Kommando 9, which was the camp dumping ground for the lowest of the low.

Then she'd find herself in a new barrack, and in her struggle to get hold of a steel bowl, a blanket, and a tiny space on a straw mat, she would feel utterly crushed and alone in the world and look back nostalgically on the peaceful infirmary, risky though it was.

I accompanied her mentally step by step through the ordeal, and over the next few days I waited eagerly for her to keep her promise and come see me. But three days passed, then four days, then two weeks, and Zina still didn't come. It was sad to feel forgotten. So she was no exception to the general rule: as soon as I was no longer part of her immediate world, I ceased to exist for her. This was natural and unavoidable and I had only myself to blame, for I couldn't help getting attached to whoever was nearby and showed me kindness. Not even in the lager could I get over this tendency.

And then the moment arrived. I knew this was bound to happen sooner or later, but that didn't make it any more tolerable. The nurse appeared, took my folder, and announced that tomorrow I would have the medical exam.

"But I've still got a fever," I objected. "How can you expect me to leave?"

"If it's not over a hundred it's not fever—it's laziness!" she snapped harshly. Once again, I was forced to accept the inevitable.

So I too passed before Dr. Koenig's myopic eyes, to be dispatched with the same ceremony. It was rather late when we left the infirmary and filed down the *Lagerstrasse*, but several Kommandos were still lined up, waiting to set off for work. I knew Kommando 9 was among the last to leave, so I looked around to see if I could spot Zinuchka. And as a matter of fact I passed right by her, but by the time I realized and turned around, she was gone. I called out several times, but she didn't seem to hear. She was trudging along bent over and looking totally defeated, in much worse shape than when I had last seen her in the infirmary.

"I told her so," I thought. "I told her she couldn't handle it."

Then I had to tend to my own affairs. The most pressing

concern of all was where I would be assigned. There was no question of my being sent to a good Kommando: being Italian as well as a fairly recent arrival, I hadn't a chance in the world of getting into Work Allocation or the Union Factory. Nevertheless, my mind kept stubbornly drifting into foolish fantasies of these aristocratic Kommandos, like those people who buy a lottery ticket and, despite all the known odds, secretly dream up an infinity of plans for the blissful life sure to await them.

Needless to say, I didn't have a winning ticket. I was sent to Kommando 9. But by then I had already reverted to the fatalism that was my sole strategy for survival. At least I would have Zina's company, I thought, which might spare me some of the bullying insolence that newcomers had to put up with.

After reporting to my new Block, I was miraculously free until evening. I stretched out on a mound of dirt at the end of the camp and tried to enjoy the sun, the puffy white clouds, the smell of the grass. I was thinking about Zina: most likely she hadn't managed to find her husband. It would take something far more cruel than fatigue to make her so downcast.

I stood in the front row for roll-call so I'd be sure to see her when Kommando 9 returned. Covered with dust, Zina was dragging herself along and would have passed by without noticing me, but I called out and she looked up. Her eyes glazed over with tears and her face was transformed, as if seeing me awakened painful memories.

"Wait for me after roll-call," I cried.

She nodded and got in line wearily, with a blank look, as though she wasn't really part of the world around her, and stood slumped over pathetically during the entire roll-call. I was even more certain she hadn't found her husband.

"Poor Zinuchka," I thought. "What a disappointment."

Finally the whistle blew and we broke ranks. I ran over to where Zina stood apart, waiting.

"Zinuchka, how are you?" I embraced her warmly. "Why didn't you come see me? I was expecting you."

She didn't answer but bent her head in a supreme effort to fight back tears.

"Well, what happened? You didn't get to see Grigori?"

I took her by the arm, and we went to sit on a pile of rocks at the end of the road. I had to keep urging before she would look up.

"Grigori's gone," she said abruptly in a strange voice, firm and yet hollow. "Grigori is dead."

"Dead!" I was shocked. "But what about the note?"

"The note was right. But it was another Szafarisc, not him."

"Well, did you see this other one? Did you talk to him?"

"Yes, I talked to him," said Zina. And growing more and more agitated, she proceeded to recount in fits and starts what must have been the most tragic scene of her life.

"I spoke to him, yes. Now you'll realize why I never came. There was no point telling something that couldn't possibly matter except to me. What is it to anyone else if Grigori is *kaputt?* Thousands of people in Birkenau are *kaputt*. In the end we'll all be *kaputt*."

She caught my slight reflexive gesture of protest and added, "I don't mean you don't care, Lianechka. But you have to understand—to leave feeling so happy and then suddenly find out that he's gone. . . . You just can't talk about it. You think to yourself, why say anything at all? It's over now, there's nothing left to say."

"But you can talk to me," I broke in, stroking her hands the way you do with children. "Tell me what happened, Zinuchka."

"What can I tell you? We got to the construction site where they're building the trenches, and this foreman I know, Vera, told me to take a wheelbarrow and cart away the dirt the men were digging up. 'That way you'll get up close and have a chance to talk,' she said. I started going back and forth with the wheelbarrow but I didn't find Grigori, so I decided to ask one of the men working nearby.

"'Where's Grigori Szafarisc? I'm his wife.'

"'Who?' the man says.

"'Grigori Szafarisc. I'm his wife!'

"'Szafarisc doesn't have any wife,' he says, very surprised, but I keep insisting, so he calls over to a young fellow a little ways off. 'Szafarisc, come over here. There's a woman who says she's your wife.'

"The man had his back to us and seemed to be built exactly like Grigori. I thought, 'In a second he's going to turn around. He'll turn, he'll see me, and he'll rush right over. Oh Zina, it's you! he'll say. Zina, Zinuchka!'

"In that one instant when I waited for him to turn, I lived through the whole scene. I had to keep myself from crying out. And then he did turn and . . ."

Zina paused, stifled a sob, and went on.

"It wasn't Grigori. He was a dark-haired fellow, and he said something to me but I couldn't register a single word. All I knew was that he wasn't Grigori. I took the wheelbarrow and left. Only later did it occur to me he might know something, so I went back.

"'Tell me,' I said, 'would you have any news of my husband?'

"'Where was he from?' he says. 'I knew a Szafarisc, but he's dead.'

"'He was from Stricwenitza. Grigori Szafarisc, from Stricwenitza—he must have been here in October.'

"'October?' he says, as if he's searching his memory.

"'He was tall, blond, with a scar on his forehead.'

"'I might have known him,' says the young man. 'It's possible, but I don't know what happened to him.'

"'What do you mean, you don't know? You said just before that he was dead!'

"Well, the fellow starts in, it's not like he really could swear to it. After that other Szafarisc went to the infirmary he didn't hear any more about him—you know how it is in the lager—but he might have gotten better. . . .''

I thought so too, and tried, out of compassion, to persuade Zina. But she had no use, now, for hopes or illusions. All she wanted was to sink quickly into darkness.

"Ah, no!" She brushed off my attempts to comfort her. "It was bad enough that I fell for it in the first place. I was a fool, don't you see? It was nothing but a hoax. This goddamned life just set me up, and I went along with the whole thing. Then when I thought I was on the verge of finding him, the joke was on me—all my efforts were for nothing. He's not even here. He's dead and gone. . . . You can't understand, you're single, you're an intellectual, you don't know what it means to live for someone else, to love him so much that he's your whole life. If he dies, your life is over— you're just going through the motions. Before, I used to haul 50 kilos of cement on my back and I hardly felt it, because I had to find Grigori. Now they could treat me like royalty, they could wine me and dine me, and I'd die just the same. I don't want to go on living—that's all there is to it."

"You mustn't say that!" I protested. "God—"

Zina cut me off with a scornful flick of the hand, so I tried another tack. "The war will be over, and then . . ."

"What do I care if the war is over? It'll always be too late for us! I don't give a damn anymore when it's over or how many people are killed."

She had gotten up and was storming about, talking very loudly. Everyone else had gone to sleep. We were alone outside in the twilight as the moon rose over the faraway hills.

"Let's go, Zina," I begged. "We have to work tomorrow."

"Good! The more they make me work, the sooner I'll die. And I'm glad, believe me."

Just then the Block sentry, who had had her eye on us for some time, came over and ordered us back in.

"I'm surprised your tongues didn't drop off, you god-damned loudmouths," she yelled, threatening us with her strap. "You like the cool air, sure, but in the morning we'll have to throw you out of bed!"

We had to obey. The nauseating air of the closed barrack, dense with the stale breath of hundreds of neglected bodies, caught in our throats.

"Good night," I said softly.

"Good night," said Zina. As I turned away, she added, "Remember, stand next to me in line tomorrow morning."

That was my first thought when I woke. I didn't leave her side for a minute during roll-call, for fear we might end up in separate groups. Finally even Kommando 9 got moving. We heard the usual sprightly marching music coming from the *Lagerstrasse,* and once past the guard post, we were on the road to the work site.

We had a long way to go. The sun shone brightly in a pale blue sky as our Kommando marched briskly past fields fragrant with hay. It was actually enjoyable, rather like a morning walk in the country. The women around me kept up a steady patter, except for Zina, morose and distracted. I kept silent so as not to get on her nerves, already worn to a frazzle: I knew from experience how exasperating other people's high spirits can be when you're trapped in your own private pain.

After close to two hours of marching we reached a large clearing where trenches and anti-aircraft emplacements were being built. Together with Zinuchka, I started heaping up dirt the men had dug up. The work didn't seem too strenuous, at least at first, and I hardly minded it. I was also keeping an eye out for any men who might speak Italian.

Dagma, our Kapo, didn't seem too bad either. She was a good-looking blond whose principal occupation was apparently laughing and bantering with two young *Posten* attached to our Kommando. They all spoke with the same easygoing southern accent, a shared idiom that erased their difference in rank, making her simply an amiable, attractive woman.

"Quick, quick, my girls! You have to earn your soup," cried Dagma, her sparkling eyes turning momentarily from the shed where the *Posten* spent their frequent breaks. Luckily she was nothing like the dreadful Kapo in Kommando 110: love made Dagma mild and merry, and I began to think the devil might not be quite the scoundrel he's made out to be.

All of a sudden the barrage balloons, like huge white sausages, rose in the sky over Auschwitz. The alarm sounded and we had to climb into the trenches.

Zinuchka and I ended up in a trench with several men, one of whom, a dark-haired young fellow, greeted her and started speaking Slavic. I had no idea what they were saying except when Zinuchka answered yes or no, but whatever the subject, the young man seemed fervently caught up. He pointed up at the sky, then out at the fields, and I soon grasped, more or less, that it must be something about guerrilla warfare, because several times I heard the word *partizan*.

"What is he saying?" I asked Zina. She told me he believed the best thing at this point would be to try to escape. The Allied advance was headed for Cracow and the whole area was surrounded by partisans; if the Germans found themselves pushed to the wall, they would definitely bomb the camp at night, slaughtering the lot of us, and blame it on the Allied Air Force. That was my opinion too, and I said so as succinctly as possible: "Absolutely — *Fritzalarm*. That's the right idea."

Indeed on that day and the days to follow, many were daring enough to find *Fritzalarm* a good idea. Every evening at roll-call the siren would blare for an escaped prisoner, proclaiming to those of us who remained that one more brave, ardent soul was racing toward freedom.

Fritzalarm, Fritzalarm! The thundering artillery came closer each day, while the thick swarms of planes buzzing through the sky above Birkenau sang out our passionate hopes. *Fritzalarm! Fritzalarm!*

I worked in the trenches while Zina pushed the wheelbarrows, but we would meet up at the soup break. Because it was so hot, we ate in the shadow of a trench wall, sharing the bits of carrot that, like buried treasure, would occasionally turn up amid the bland white turnip soup.

Ivan, the young man who had known Grigori, would stop by now and then to say hello to Zina, and she seemed to welcome his company, which was encouraging. Now that the worst was over, I thought, she would gradually recover her will to live. What worried me more was her health — she seemed weaker each day, as if her meager energies were draining away.

"You have a fever," I said, touching her warm forehead. "You ought to go to the infirmary. You can't keep this up."

But Zina shook her head and said she was doing fine: helping Ivan took her mind off things. One day she mended his jacket; another time she gave him some pumpkin seeds and peelings she'd riskily gathered from the garbage.

"I feel like I'm doing it for Grigori, don't you see?" said Zina. "They were together, and it feels like part of him lives on in Ivan. . . ."

There came a day when I overheard her humming a Russian folk song, another favorite of mine.

"It's my song," said Zinuchka. I asked her to sing it for me again.

> With the last of my fortune, my five-ruble note
> I'll hire me a troika with horses of white.
> I'll give all I have to the driver and say:
> Brother, go fast as you can, fly away!

"Why is it your song?" I asked, not getting the connection.

"Because I want to spend my last five rubles fast, just like that. When you haven't much left and you're going to lose it anyway, why be thrifty? Better to toss it all away on some grand gesture, serve some purpose."

I remarked that there wasn't much opportunity for grand gestures in the lager; if you behaved magnanimously, you were simply taken for a fool and reaped nothing but scorn and abuse.

But Zina said that wasn't the point at all. The point was to be generous with your tiny hoard, be useful to someone, like the spendthrift of the song. He knows he's got nothing left, he's practically drunk on his own impending doom, so he chooses a magnificent troika and gives everything he has to the driver.

"And then the game is up," Zina concluded, hiding something in her breast.

I was curious. "What have you got there? Did Vera give you some peelings?"

"No, no, it's something of Ivan's," she said warily. "Cigarettes."

"Why did he give them to you? Does he want you to trade them for bread?"

"No, for a jacket."

Since it was hardly chilly, I wondered why anyone would want a jacket rather than bread. Zina confided that Ivan couldn't look for a civilian jacket without arousing suspicion, but she knew a girl in Work Allocation who could get hold of one easily in exchange for cigarettes.

"What if there's an inspection? What'll you do if they find a civilian jacket under your dress?"

Zina smiled. "The most they can do is kill me."

"I could understand if you were taking this kind of chance for your husband. But after all, what's Ivan to you? Nothing."

"Nothing, that's true. But Grigori died here and I'll die here too. If Ivan does manage to get away, he'll come back to fight, and he'll be fighting for us too, you see? Even if we're gone by then, at least we'll have someone taking our revenge on these goddamned bastards."

I had nothing to say to that. A few days later I saw Zina looking plumper, and despite the heat, her sleeves were down and her collar buttoned up tight.

"You've got the jacket, don't you?" I said. "Change places with me. You stand in an inside row. You'll be safer when we pass the inspection post."

Her roomy dress covered everything just fine. No one would ever have noticed without looking closely. But I've never been able to relax when I'm involved in something surreptitious: I held my breath until we were past the gate and far from any possible inspection.

"Watch out for the *Posten*," I warned, pointing out an old soldier only recently arrived, who was the worst of all. A wizened little man with a spiteful jaundiced face, he was clearly a fanatic, impelled to give vent to his wicked instincts. He was forever prowling around the trenches, accompanied by a huge German shepherd as ferocious as its master, and he was afflicted with a peculiar phobia: he couldn't abide any conversation between the men and women. This was officially prohibited, but since they worked side by side, they naturally managed to get in a few words here and there. People said that when this guard caught any men with their *kochani* he would set the pack of dogs on them, to rip them to shreds, and these stories gave a certain chill to the air when the fiendish old man was around.

We reached the clearing and got to work. The morning passed calmly, but then toward noon the barrage balloons

rose over Auschwitz again, making everyone snort in vexation: the alarm would no doubt go off right at the soup break,
and if it continued long enough we'd miss the break and
have to resign ourselves to working on an empty stomach
until late in the evening. This had been happening for quite
a while now—couldn't the Allies have chosen a more convenient moment?

Sure enough, on this particular day, it went off punctually. By now it was practically routine, though: no sooner
had the planes passed than the *Posten* yelled at us to get right
back to work—quick, quick, quick!—as if the outcome of
the war depended solely on those four trenches. I was just
picking up my shovel when I noticed the old *Posten* staring
keenly over toward the nearest trench. His face turned savage
as he brandished his club.

"Why aren't you where you belong?" he screamed. "What
were you doing down there? You like to talk to the men,
eh? You think you're still back in the whorehouse?"

As Zina climbed up out of the trench I saw at once that
she had delivered the jacket.

"So you like to hang around the men!" he shouted again,
with his demonic glare. "You forget this is a lager! We don't
need any whores here!"

And raising his club, he began beating Zina furiously on
the chest and shoulders. The blows were so fierce that in
her frail state she collapsed instantly. He kept on beating her
as she lay there on the ground, while the dog leaped about,
barking eagerly, ready to tear her limb from limb.

"Back to work, hurry up, scram!" he yelled, adding one
last kick as a measure of his scorn. Then he turned to the
rest of us, but as always in such cases, everyone was busy

grabbing a hoe or shovel and hurrying back to work with quite incredible alacrity. I was right opposite Zina but didn't dare go to her aid. I was well aware that helping someone who had been punished was an infraction of the rules, liable to the same savage retribution. I simply didn't dare. It was pure torment to see my friend flat on her back and bleeding, and yet I didn't make a move, for fear of the club. Chafing inwardly, I went about my work, not venturing a step outside the trench.

After lying very still for a long time, Zina finally stirred. I took advantage of a moment when the *Posten* was out of sight to dash over.

"Come on, Zinuchka, try to get up," I pleaded. "Make an effort. If the *Posten* comes back and finds you here he'll beat you again."

"I can't," she moaned. "It hurts so, I can't move. Let me die in peace."

"You have to get up," I insisted. "You have to! Please try, Zinuchka."

I took hold of her arms and pulled her to her feet, but as soon as she was upright, her knees buckled and she sank back down.

"I can't move," she groaned. "Go back to work and stop torturing me. Let me die in peace. Go away."

It seemed cruel to persist but I did. Finally I realized it was no use and returned to the trench.

After a while Zina's friend Vera, the foreman, came to see why she wasn't back on her feet. She too tried to get her to move, at least a couple of steps to the nearest trench: if the *Posten* came back and found her lying there, she'd be in more trouble. With her powerful arms, Vera gripped her by the waist, hoisting her up and dragging her along. But after a few steps Zina stopped. She seemed to be choking.

"Hey, what's with you?" said Vera. "How about if you had been punished with the twenty-five blows like I was? Come on now, enough of this!"

Suddenly she jerked out of the way as Zina heaved and a stream of blood gushed from her mouth. She fell to the ground, choking and writhing.

"Water! Bring some water!" cried Vera. People ran to fetch some, but water was so scarce in Birkenau that no one could find any. It was quite a while before one man came back with a bit of turnip broth strained into a metal bowl.

"Drink, you'll feel better." I tried to slide a few drops into Zina's mouth. I had to keep wiping her lips, which were bright red, for the bleeding wouldn't let up. She stared straight ahead, unaware, desiring nothing more, her features razor-sharp as the color drained from her face.

Meanwhile, the Kapo had gone to ask one of the *Posten* what to do: the woman seemed very ill. What if she died before we got back to the lager?

"So you'll carry her on your back," he replied, scowling. "My job is to bring back the whole Kommando. Dead or alive, I don't give a damn."

So that was that. We resumed our work, and Zina lay on the ground, her head resting on a stone. I ran over whenever I could to see how she was. After a while she seemed to grow drowsy, and as the day wore on without further incident, her face became so gray and the shadows around her eyes so deep that the women were taking bets on whether or not she'd make it to the lager. Most of them figured she'd wind up *kaputt* along the road.

When the final whistle blew, Zina was lifted onto a makeshift stretcher some women had woven together out of branches.

"Go slow," she moaned in a bare sliver of a voice. "Slow down, it hurts."

She was bleeding from the mouth again, but the Kapo, the guards, and Vera kept rushing us along. Hurry up, they said, we had a long walk, we were late already, they couldn't bother about Zinuchka right now.

At long last the stretcher lurched its way to the gate, where the officer on duty took one look at Zina and asked what happened.

"*Kaputt* on the job, Sir," replied the Kapo with a smile. With a wave of his pencil, the officer had us march on without breaking stride.

As always, ours was the last Kommando to return; the others were already in formation and the *blockowa* came forward, quite irate.

"We have a very sick woman here, *Frau blockowa*," said the Kapo, setting the stretcher on the ground. "We need to get her to the infirmary right away. She's really bad. She was bleeding from the mouth."

"What do you mean, the infirmary right away!" exclaimed the *blockowa*. She was genuinely horror-struck. "It's roll-call. You can't take anyone anywhere! You'll call for the ambulance later."

"She's too sick to wait till later. She could die any minute!"

"It can't be done! Absolutely not!" growled the *blockowa*. And since an auxiliary was approaching, she raised her club to wave us back to our places.

So Zina stayed where she was. It never failed: the more desperate we were for roll-call to go quickly, the longer it took. The auxiliary counted wrong and had to do it over twice, and then the *Lagerführer* turned up. We were still in line when the mournful *Fritzalarm* sliced through the tranquil evening air. There was a subdued murmur — *Fritzalarm! Fritzalarm!* — and we all instinctively looked out toward the countryside, where the distant hills merged in a violet shadow.

Off in a corner, abandoned on her stretcher, Zina opened her eyes as if she wanted to say something. The auxiliary was gone, so I left the ranks and ran to her.

"*Fritzalarm*, Zinuchka." I bent down and stroked her hair. "Can you hear it? Are you content now?"

Zina nodded, straining to raise her head and speak, but her voice was so cracked and faint that I had to lean down to her lips to catch it.

"The bill —" I could barely make out her words. "The five-ruble bill . . ."

"What bill, Zinuchka?"

But Zina spoke no more. As the echo of the *Fritzalarm* vanished into air, she fell back down, her eyes closing.

*Scheiss Egal**

*Who gives a shit?,
or, more literally,
the same old shit.
—Tr. note

For three days now I had been working in the infirmary's Kitchen Squad, and each night I woke in a cold sweat, terrified of losing this precious job. I hadn't had a comparable stroke of luck since I'd been in the lager, and given the scheme of things, I most likely never would again.

Twice a day I brought the soup to the infirmary, which meant bending over, puffing and panting under heavy iron vats brimming with boiling hot broth. But then the rest of the day was gloriously free. In good weather I could sit in some out of the way corner, hidden from the road, or when it rained, take refuge in the warmth of the latrines.

Each morning I stood at the kitchen door, balancing the long, heavy crossbars of the vat on my shoulders, as my old Kommando passed by. "Still with the *Esskolonne?*" Stella and Jeannette and Cucciolo would call out, and I would beam smugly, full of self-importance, and call back, "Still with the *Esskolonne!*"

Then, along with my partner, Marianne, I would hoist up the vats and haul them across the lager to the cluster of barracks that made up the infirmary. It wasn't a long trip, but we needed to stop to change hands and catch our breath every twenty steps or so. Marianne regularly blamed me for every pause, though she was obviously panting and struggling as much as I.

Once we made it to a barrack we could take it easy until the empty vats were returned. From the doorway we peered in at the long, narrow ward, poorly lit by open skylights, as countless lackluster eyes peered back from all along the three tiers of bunk beds. In the aisle between the double row of bunks stood an all-purpose little counter: first thing in the morning, the patients set their washing buckets on it, and then later on doctors making their rounds used it to line up the medications; at last, when there was no danger of being caught, it was a convenient perch for patients who feared their muscles would atrophy from staying in bed. There they sat talking over the events of the day, like villagers congregating on the low walls around the churchyard on mild, quiet evenings.

Those of us in the *Esskolonne* were strictly forbidden to enter the wards, and the nurses pushed us around roughly when they found us at a patient's bed. Nevertheless, there were always greetings and messages to pass on or errands to carry out for someone or other. Very often the patients themselves besieged us with such a multitude of urgent requests that we were overwhelmed and, unable to grant them all, would simply cut and run before some furious nurse attacked.

That September morning—the fourth of my illustrious service in the Infirmary *Esskolonne*—I was in the doorway of the Block 9 ward waiting for the vats to be returned, when a feeble voice, coughing and straining to be heard, called out anxiously in typical lager style, "Hey you! Hey you!"

I looked around. The voice came from low down, from one of the horrid, dark bunks that were practically at floor level, smothered by the mat above, where the nurses customarily put those patients who were too weak to protest.

I couldn't make out who was lying there in the shadows, and so after checking to see that Hanka wasn't around—the burly, tough nurse who liked to rough people up—I went over.

"Liana. Aren't you Liana, the Italian?" came a painfully weak voice.

"Yes, I'm Liana."

I had no recollection whatsoever of the waxen-faced girl gaping dolefully out at me from the depths of the dark cubbyhole. With indifference, I examined the wasted, consumptive face, which seemed carved by the large, clear grayblue eyes. This young girl must be quite sick, I thought, but her condition was fairly standard for the infirmary and no longer affected me in the least. Rather, I searched my memory to recall how I knew her, but turned up nothing.

"You're Liana," the girl repeated. "I slept next to you in the quarantine barrack, remember? I used to lend you my pocket-knife to cut your bread. Don't you remember?"

And then it dawned on me. I could see it all vividly—the suffocating quarantine barrack, and Lotti and Gustine, the sweet Dutch sisters who never refused me their pocket-knife and were so discreet about asking for it back when I kept it too long.

"Gustine!" I cried, consciously suppressing my spontaneous reaction: God Almighty, you look dreadful!

But Gustine could tell and turned away with a knowing look of chagrin. Her hands, nearly transparent, lay limp on the gray blanket.

"I'm *kaputt*," she said. "I'll never get back home."

This was my feeling as well, but naturally I resorted to the usual stale assurances: we were all *kaputt*, we had to keep up our courage and hold out just a little longer, it would all be over soon.

"Do you really think the war will be over by Christmas?"

Gustine broke in, pushing herself up from the mat. The question might have been doubtful, and yet the poor doomed eyes fervently implored: "Say it will be over. Say that by Christmas the war will be over!"

In truth, I needed to believe it too, maybe a good deal more than my pride would let me acknowledge. And so I asserted confidently that not only would the war be over, but by Christmas we'd be sleeping and eating in the comfort of home, enjoying ourselves around a warm stove. I even repeated the report from the camp radio, which had been circulating for some time. "The Russians are a hundred twenty kilometers away. Don't you hear the cannon fire at night?"

Yes, Gustine too had heard the distant rumble of shots echoing from beyond the pale hills that surrounded the dreary Silesian plains. And seeing how she brightened up at the mere mention of this, I realized it was that remote rumbling, with its promise of salvation, that was keeping her barely alive.

"The doctor reads the papers," whispered Gustine, as if letting me in on a priceless secret, "and she said it'll all be over in two weeks."

I had been hearing that line for four months and would endure the equivocal pleasure of hearing it for still another year. But just now I could only brighten up too and promise to visit Gustine in Holland.

"Would you sing me that song about the golden ring?" I asked. This was a popular tune I used to love to hear both sisters sing. "Who first taught it to me, you or Lotti?" By the way, I added, if she had any message for her sister, I'd be glad to pass it on. Oh, and apropos of work, was Lotti still in that miserable sewer Kommando?

"No," replied Gustine, and to my surprise her face abruptly took on a strange look of repugnance and pain, such as when you touch a red-hot iron. This was odd, but since I had no idea what might have provoked it, I went on and asked whether her sister ever came to see her. The best time to sneak into the barrack was in the morning, before roll-call, when the night nurse was still half-asleep. Did Lotti know that?

There was a strained silence, in which Gustine seemed to be grappling with warring impulses. "No," she said finally. "Lotti's gone. Lotti is dead."

"Dead?" I was shocked. I remembered Gustine's sister very well, an attractive blond girl with a bright, appealing face. She had seemed so strong and healthy. How could she be dead?

"She's dead, I'm telling you," said Gustine. And drawing back into the shadows, she covered her face and curled herself up in a ball, weeping and coughing violently.

I leaned down and tried to console her: think of how poor Lotti up in heaven must feel, seeing her carry on that way— for even I was capable of mentioning heaven, when it was a matter of comforting a weeping friend and I could find no valid earthly rationalizations. But Gustine kept crying and coughing even harder, half-stifled under the blanket, and just then, the colossal Hanka swept over me like a tornado. She hurled me violently into the washroom, tossing me back and forth against the empty vats and screaming that I was the filthiest whore she had ever laid eyes on.

I rushed away, along with Marianne, a cold, rude Dane who spoke such a rapid, guttural German that I never understood a word she said. Nonetheless, she did manage to make certain essential things clear, yelling as if I were deaf and scornfully calling me "macaroni" when, in her opinion, I wasn't holding up my end of the vat.

Outside, the weather wasn't bad. As the dense early morning fog lifted, the sky showed a pale blue, with scattered billowy clouds. All the old-timers were predicting an unusually mild, clear autumn. In past years, they said, the camp had been deep in snow by this time, and people were already freezing to death in their icy little crannies.

"God is helping us," one or another of them would declare, eyeing the horizon.

I always felt like asking why God would help us in particular and allow last year's unfortunate souls to freeze to death, but besides the fact that people in the lager don't care to have their wisdom disputed, there was always the chance they might be right after all, in which case it was better to keep quiet and not make waves, as it were. The sun was shining, which was all to the good: better not to probe so deeply.

As I walked, I kept thinking of poor Lotti. There was that evening I had spent regaling her with descriptions of the sun and skies of Italy and the perfumed streets of the Riviera, where olive and pine trees curved gently over the small coves, and the water was so clear and limpid that the stones at the bottom glistened in reflected sunlight.

"How wonderful!" Lotti had cried, spellbound. "It sounds so wonderful!" And she vowed to come visit me in Italy. I was delighted. I no longer had a house to return to, and yet I was happily planning to welcome her with lavish hospitality.

Ah, poor Lotti! I sighed and sang a bit of the song she always used to sing:

Once I had a golden ring,
A golden ring my love gave me . . .

Marianne turned in annoyance, yelling at me to keep quiet. Granted, I didn't sing very well, but that didn't give her the right to stop me. Even people who are tone-deaf get the urge to sing once in a while, especially when they're lonely and the song on their lips releases their deepest heartache.

So Lotti had gone up in smoke, never again to sing the song about the golden ring. But why did Gustine look so strange at the mention of her name?

Most of the sisters in the camp loved each other with an almost morbid attachment, and possibly Gustine, sick as she was, felt her sister's death all the more. I brooded over the troubling episode until we reached the kitchens, where I lined up the vats at the door, then ran to my usual corner.

The piles of rocks behind Block 5 made it a strategic location as well as a gathering place: you had a view of the *Lagerstrasse* while remaining safely hidden. Today I said hello to a group of talkative Greek women from the latest transports, sitting in a tight jabbering circle.

At this time of day, only those people from the quarantine barrack were around the camp. Nearly all the Kommandos were off at work, and the few people passing along the *Lagerstrasse* were sweepers, for the most part, bored with pretending to clean an already immaculate road. They would wander by from time to time yawning, but always alert enough to pick up some stray leaf or pebble if a soldier came along, or if the *Lagerkapo*'s dread silhouette appeared on the horizon.

I couldn't get the song about the golden ring out of my mind. The warm sun felt good on my closed eyes as I listened to the words going round and round in my head. All of a sudden a pebble hit me right on the knee and a lively voice exhorted me in rather Frenchified German: "*Arbeit! Arbeit! Los, los, Arbeit!* Get moving, you old cow!"

I smiled. That was Rosette, a tiny woman from Marseilles who was attached to some minor inside Kommando that was barely supervised. Rosette the *débrouillard* (operator) managed to sneak away from work briefly every day to come and keep me company. She was cunning and malicious as a monkey, which she actually resembled — swift, restless movements and shrewd little eyes that didn't miss a trick. She came from the *vieux port* of Marseilles and enjoyed some notoriety as a troublemaker, yet I found her good company: I liked listening to her rattle away in her rapid-fire style, with all sorts of colorful exclamations thrown in.

Rosette sat down and announced that the Russians were a hundred fifty kilometers away: in two weeks it would all be over. "*Oh, bonne Mère, bonne Mère!*" she sighed impatiently, scratching an open sore on her right leg.

"Did you know that Lotti, the little Dutch girl, is dead?" I said, merely to contribute my own news. "I saw her sister in the infirmary. She won't be around much longer herself, I don't think."

"Lotti, you mean the one from the quarantine Block?" snapped Rosette in a challenging tone. "Who told you she's dead?"

"Her sister did, just this morning. Why, what's so funny about that?"

"Ah, my dear girl," Rosette went on, as if it were a point

of honor to contradict me. "Anything but dead! She's in better shape than we are. I wouldn't mind stuffing my face the way she is. Her sister may go up the chimney, but whores always have all the luck."

"Whores?" I was thunderstruck. And yet it explained that puzzling, stricken look on Gustine's face when she heard her sister's name. Yes, Rosette's words were clearing up the mystery.

"You said it!" She spoke with the vindictive spite that poor and respectable women customarily feel toward those who are well-off and somewhat less chaste. "Lotti signed up for the Auschwitz *Puffkommando* (brothel), and from then on her sister said she was dead, she didn't want anything more to do with her. That's why she told you that. She won't take anything from her, and she has a fit when Lotti sends her things."

I wanted to hear more of this intriguing story, but Rosette spied her Kapo off in the distance and had to rush back to work. I stayed on alone, amid the incessantly chattering Greeks. The noon hour came and went. When it was almost four, I reported to the kitchens to take the ersatz tea to the infirmary. Marianne, who was already there, warned me in her usual nasty way not to go into the ward again.

"Mind your own business and leave me alone," was what I wanted to say. But since those phrases were too complex for my German, I just shrugged disdainfully and we set off.

It was the same old routine, putting one foot in front of the other. Everything is forever the same in the lager, piti-lessly, hopelessly the same; each hour brings the same acts, the same commands, the same everything, until soon even your thoughts take the same predictable track, making the same fixed stops—the war, home, getting back—a chronic sameness that becomes a torture worthy of Dante. At a certain bend in the road I would see a clump of grass sprouting between two rocks; it took fifty steps to get there. Each day, twice a day, I counted the steps and looked for the grass, and then I looked at the little poplars along the wide, well-trodden *Lagerstrasse* and thought invariably of how few of the people who had planted them two or three years ago were still around to watch their young leaves stirring.

I didn't dare enter Gustine's ward, since the fearful Hanka was in the vicinity. Instead, I inquired of a Ukrainian woman who slept in the bunk above and happened to be in the doorway getting some fresh air, her blanket wrapped around her infirmary-style.

"*Kaputt,* completely *kaputt!*" replied the Ukrainian with scorn, for she was quite robust—she just had a sore eye. "All night long she moans. I can't sleep a wink. If she keeps it up, Hanka's sure to smack her around."

I had a feeling the Ukrainian herself would smack Gustine around if she lost any more sleep, so I tried to make excuses, saying it was the fever.

"You girls always have a fever," the Ukrainian retorted, and she spat on the ground to illustrate her disgust for the feverish.

The next day I had better luck and managed to get inside. Gustine was obviously worse. She lay flat on her back, her face flushed and sweating. The moment she saw me, though, she roused herself and reached for my hand.

"Did you hear the artillery last night?" she asked, first thing. And without waiting for a reply, as if pursuing an obsessive inner dialogue, she rushed on, "If they keep advancing at this rate, it'll be over in even less than two weeks. We'll be home way before Christmas. And you know," she kept on, clearing her throat, "it's cold in my country. At home we'll have all the stoves going."

I told her to keep still, because talking seemed to wear her out, but Gusti paid no attention. She told me all about home, the way she used to do in the quarantine Block. She could go on about it for hours on end, with almost lyrical descriptions of the fire sparkling in the big blue tiled stove and her mother preparing the snacks for tea, the smell of fresh bread, the most comforting smell in the world, and the butter, the ruby-hued currant marmalade, the gaily colored curtains on the windows. Oh, beloved home, the most cherished place on earth!

As I listened, the Dutch family's cheerful house sprang vividly to life, symbolizing everything in the world now lost, banished, destroyed. I pictured Gusti sitting near the radio and Lotti studying her Latin . . . then all at once Rosette and the Auschwitz *Puff* were superimposed on those tranquil images, obliterating them. I was back on the ward, in the depressing Birkenau infirmary—a stroke of luck, actually, since I caught sight of Hanka in time to make a getaway. Before I left I assured Gustine I'd see her soon.

"Come back tomorrow," she called. In a manner of speaking, that is—for, really, she didn't have the strength to call anything.

I woke the next morning in a bad mood. For as long as I can remember, I have been superstitious, not only keeping track of commonplace instances of fate, but analyzing my dreams in scrupulous detail, in order to coax out any hidden warnings from beyond. That morning I woke with the sense

of a confused dream, but its bad omens were clear enough.
It seemed Gustine had given me flowers (flowers mean sorrow); I was in a beautiful house, sitting beside a big blue
tiled stove, eating sweets (sweets mean bitterness), and I lost
a tooth (losing a tooth means very bad luck). The import of
this dream was plain as day and anything but reassuring. I
told Cucciolo and Jeannette and Rosette, who agreed that it
boded no good.

To start a day knowing it will end badly can hardly be
called encouraging, and yet I prefer to be strategically fore-
warned, so I can anticipate the wide range of possible
disasters and inure myself in advance; in this way, I can
dilute their power and arrive at a sage indifference. What
could happen to me? Would my bread be stolen, would I
be beaten? There was always the chance of an impromptu
selection. I could be sent to the crematorium. All in all,
though, the most likely and most distressing event would be
to lose my precious job with the *Esskolonne*.

I waited for roll-call with my heart in my throat. Only
when I heard my name called as usual could I breathe easily
and proceed calmly to the kitchens. Leaning against the wall,
I watched the last Kommandos file by on their way to work:
the Union factory "Bluecaps" were setting off for the day
shift, while the "Redheads" of the Work Allocation Kommando, buxom, well-dressed girls, straggled back from their
night work: lucky creatures! As they passed the kitchens, one
girl broke out of line and came running over. "Anyone going
to Block 9 of the infirmary?" she hurriedly asked.

"I am," I said.

The Redhead handed me a little package. For Gustine
. . . from her sister, she said. Meanwhile her Kapo wagged

a warning finger. "*Pass auf!* Better watch your step," she said sternly, but the girl wasn't the least bit disturbed. The Kapo and her subordinates in the rich Work Allocation Kommando were allied in a freemasonry of the common good, unlike our impoverished Kommandos, where absurd, unbridgeable chasms divided the Kapo from the irredeemable proletariat.

Needless to say, I was quite curious to see what was in the package and looked inside. Sticking up among a dozen or so cigarettes, the most coveted treasure in the camp, was a note: "Dear Gusti, I know you're sick and I'm sending these cigarettes so you can buy yourself something. Please let me know how you are. Your sister, Lotti."

It was written in pencil, evidently in haste, in the sort of tall, angular handwriting that some young girls find elegant. "It's scented!" cried the woman behind me, who had leaned over to translate.

Of course everyone had to smell the perfume, so the note was passed around and sniffed ecstatically. I smelled it too — just the faintest breath of scent, as if the paper had been near face powder. Still, I pressed it close to my nostrils and inhaled greedily. Just then a Kapo came out of the kitchen, surprised to find us still there.

"What is it? What's going on now? What are you old bitches up to!" she screeched in the usual lager way.

"Perfume, *Frau* Kapo." Marianne smiled maliciously, nodding toward me.

The Kapo didn't bother with me, though. I was much too bedraggled to be accused of "organizing." She pushed us aside, still yelling, "What's going on, what's going on?" and we shouldered the vats and set out.

Along the way I kept glancing down at my pocket, where Gustine's treasure was hidden, and imagining what those cigarettes could mean to me in terms of food. One cigarette was worth six or seven potatoes, plus half a ration of bread. If I took just a handful, I'd have three or four bowlfuls of delicious hot yellow potatoes, maybe with a little onion. Anyone who has ever been in a lager, condemned to turnip soup, knows the kind of agonized yearning this image can call forth.

My fantasies got so acute that I was in a frenzy of temptation and cast about for some notion that might help me resist. For instance, maybe Gustine was dead, in which case I would become the legitimate possessor of all the cigarettes. Or maybe she wouldn't want them or would decide to present me with a few, as a token of gratitude. One way or another, I was convinced I couldn't possibly come away with nothing and was already planning to have Jeannette handle the deal for me, since I've never been adept at business matters and was even less so in the lager, where need elicits unsuspected and quite terrifying capacities for extortion.

It was a relief to get to the infirmary, for the struggle between my urge to seize a share of the treasure and my scruples about a deed so alien to my pre-lager training was assuming the proportions of a conflict between virtue and vice.

I managed to slip into the ward, where I found Gustine stretched out unconscious on her mat, motionless as a corpse, her face looking chiseled in wax. "Gustine," I called hesitantly. I asked the Ukrainian, who was poking her head out from the bunk above, whether Gustine was sleeping, but she merely shrugged.

"Gustine!" I called again, bending over to stroke her smooth brown hair, drenched with sweat. "Are you asleep, Gustine?"

Finally she came to. She seemed to open her eyes with effort, and her face had that look of pained stupor so common among the dying: they gaze all around slowly, in bewilderment, maybe even disappointed to find themselves still here.

"Look, Gustine, these are to buy yourself some warm milk for your bread." I put the little package in her hand. "There's a note, too." Gusti clutched the paper and stared as though my words came from a great distance and she didn't quite grasp their meaning.

I was afraid to upset her by mentioning Lotti's name, yet I didn't know what kind of story to invent. "One of the Redheads gave it to me," I said as a last resort, and I dabbed away the sweat on Lotti's sister's brow.

"*She* gave it to you?" she burst out, with an energy I could hardly believe. Again there was that frightened look of disgust. "She knows I don't want her things! I don't want anything from her, do you understand?"

She grabbed the package and hurled it violently across the room. It struck a corner of the counter, the wrapping opened, and the cigarettes rolled out and scattered on the floor. Gustine looked at them for a moment, then fell back in a torrent of weeping. Great silent tears gushed out, dripping on to her dirty shirt.

Meanwhile the Ukrainian leaped down from her bunk, followed by another patient, and then another. Quick as a flash, a horde of crazed women were scrambling around on the floor, yelling and cursing, tearing the crumbling, but no less coveted, cigarettes from each other's hands. The patients at the far end of the ward sat up to ask what was happening, Gustine wept silently, and I, like a fool, stood at her bed, paralyzed by a sense of impending doom, as a troop of raging nurses led by Hanka and the *blockowa* stormed in. Terrified, the crowd of women took flight, scattering in every direction. As if in a dream, I saw the Ukrainian's thick white legs fly over my head as she darted back to her bunk.

"It's her! It's her every time! This time I'll take care of you myself, you filthy slut!" screamed Hanka, falling on me and attacking wildly, hurling blows every which way. My face burned as I struggled to escape, but her hands gripped my neck like a vice. Dragging me across the room, she flung me before the *blockowa* like a sinner cast into the presence of our Lord on Judgment Day.

The woman in charge of Block 9 was a beautiful young Slovak, always impeccably turned out, who would generally attend to the Block a half-hour before the German doctor came by on his rounds. The patients said she wasn't bad-natured and maybe that was so; she was too self-absorbed, in any event, to spare the time required to be bad-natured. She would most often be seen passing through the ward with the serene bearing of the oblivious, on her way to take a hot bath with the water delivered for tea. There was nothing especially shocking about this, it was the law of the lager, and in her place we would surely have done the same. Today, however, the barrack's normal routine had been disrupted, and the young *blockowa* promptly demonstrated her outrage at this affront to her personal tranquillity by giving me two smacks. Then she fingered the small rectangular label on my dress with my registration number and compared it with the number tattooed on my arm. And shoving me contemptuously back to Hanka, she strolled off regally, an unruffled guardian of justice.

Hanka grabbed me and beat me again. It was quite a while before she had had enough and let me go. Back in the washroom Marianne stood waiting with the empty vats, regarding me with vicious delight.

"If she took your number," she hastened to inform me, enunciating clearly to make sure I understood, "if she took your number it means you'll be sent to the *Strafkommando.*"

I couldn't care less, at that moment, about being sent to the Punishment Kommando. All I could register was that Marianne had two cigarettes hidden in the hem of her dress. I was flooded with rage. I wanted to lunge at her and yank out her hair, draw blood, trample her underfoot as I had so often seen others do, tear her virtually limb from limb.

"*Schweine!*" I said with a murderous glance.

"*Schweine* to you too!" Marianne replied coolly, getting a grip on the vat.

I had no choice but to help her. My face was on fire and I could feel it swelling up as I walked. Gradually my rage dissipated, and in its place came a terror of what might happen. I would be severely punished, that was certain. I might very well be sent to the *Strafkommando.* I could see myself with the red circle on my back and my hair all shorn again. I would be utterly lost, for the Punishment Kommando was made up almost entirely of Poles, Ukrainians, and, worst of all, German ex-Kapos, whose motto was the harshest law of the lager: Make the weak your slaves; keep them down by force.

It was sad indeed, trudging for the last time down those familiar paths. The infirmary and its surroundings—all those things never to be seen again in quite that way, at that time of day—took on the melancholy charm of leavetaking: the sentries sitting at the barrack doors like concierges at the entrances of their buildings, a few doctors passing the time of day, the white-uniformed nurses chattering gaily, carrying litters for the dead. Everything touched me, everything spoke in a plangent tone of lament. Never again would I cross that road carrying vats of soup. And those piercing words, "never again," contained all the tragedy of the irreparable.

Feeling utterly despondent, I set down the vats at the kitchen door and went silently to my usual corner. I couldn't even take solace in Rosette's company. For as often happens in life, my misfortune simply served to bolster her sense of superiority, her greater presence of mind. She wouldn't have allowed herself to be beaten by Hanka; she would never have let that piggish Marianne get away with two cigarettes. "*Oh, merde alors!*" Rosette cried with sparkling eyes, making me feel weaker and lonelier than ever.

The next morning I waited until the last possible moment to line up with the other women in the *Esskolonne*. Their frank stares made me even more uneasy. I knew they were waiting to see me publicly disgraced.

They didn't have very long to wait. The Kapo came over immediately and took me by the arm, and with the irrevocable words, "Get away, you! Scram!" threw me out of the *Esskolonne* squad.

I slunk away, swallowing the words, bitter as gall, that I had painstakingly prepared. To protest, or even to plead, would obviously be of no avail. The ill omens of my dream the other night had come true.

Now I was resigned to the worst and went to the reserve line expecting to be called to the *Strafkommando*. But fate came to my aid: I was sent to a group assigned to various drudgeries, more tedious than difficult. It was a matter of traipsing around carrying rocks, sacks, and clods of earth from here to there in long processions, and I was glad enough to be doing it. The great benefit of being prepared for the worst is that the merely bad always seems a blessing.

What with one chore after another, a week or so went by, and I was used to the new routines. Generally we would start out at the station, but then one morning they took us to the far end of the lager where the linens were stored. Beside a truck heaped with blankets stood a pompous, pot-bellied auxiliary, all decked out in ribbons and medals and nicknamed Goeringuska, by virtue of her resemblance to the Nazi leader. Two women from the laundry were poised on top of the truck, and as we filed by below, they tossed four or five blankets down to each of us. When that was done, Goeringuska counted us and the blankets twice and ordered our Kapo to follow an escort *Posten* and make it quick: oh, she knew that lazy devils like us could take hours to go to Auschwitz, but if we weren't back soon, she'd personally see to it that we were sorry.

"Now step on it, *los!*"

An animated murmur spread through the lines. Heads bobbed eagerly beneath the blankets. Most of us had never been to Auschwitz, and in the lager, any novelty is cause for excitement.

Once we were past the gates, going from Birkenau to the town, we didn't even feel the weight of the blankets, we were so enraptured. The road itself offered nothing of any interest. Quite the contrary, it was a humble carriage-road cutting through the fields. The fascination lay simply in its being a genuine *road* — ordinary people, bicycles, or village carts might pass by. We were accustomed to the lager roads, girded and restricted by barbed wire and guard towers, while this "real" road had no beginning or end in sight and wended its way across fields, over bridges, through towns: truly the open road of legend.

Auschwitz was about five kilometers away: we noted this on a traffic sign, another curious novelty. Life in the lager had made us regress to a weird, alienated sort of infancy, shut off from every sign of common civilian life. Everything we saw intrigued us. Like innocent, raw country children, we marveled, we were thrilled and impressed.

"The train, the train!" cried one woman as we passed below a trestle bridge. Even the Kapo stopped to gaze, enthralled, at the train whizzing by on gleaming tracks.

Then came the town — rows of dark, dismal, two- and three-story houses with sloping roofs, surrounded by damp, hushed green gardens. Along the avenues, which were paved like certain Roman streets, strolled people dressed in a peculiar antiquated style, rather like the eccentric English tourists pictured in turn-of-the-century newspapers. The citizenry of Auschwitz — worried-looking, dingy, blond, and unappealing — were evidently not in high spirits.

To the left, a little ways outside the town, was the men's lager, and above its huge wrought-iron gate hung the camp motto: "*Arbeit macht frei.*" Work brings freedom. We laughed and chorused the well-known lager saying: "Work, work will make you free, Crematorium, one two three." The Kapo paused so that the old guard who was lagging behind could catch up, and we entered the camp, passing by the guard corps, a throng of jolly young soldiers busy cleaning their guns or smoking their pipes.

The lager wasn't half bad. Compared to the filthy barracks at Birkenau, it struck us as almost magnificent. Instead of barracks there were actual houses, quite clean-looking and, wonder of wonders, each of them boasting a little front garden! Only a few measly flower-beds, but they were lovingly tended—pansies, pink carnations, and even some tomato plants bearing glossy red fruits.

Even in Auschwitz, it was clear the men were treated better than the women; we couldn't help taking offense. "Oh, men," we groaned with mingled scorn and envy, but our complaints were cut short as the Kapo divided us into groups and handed us over to more guards, who would supervise the distribution of the blankets.

Since my group was one of the first to finish, we stood waiting on the street, studying everything in sight, waving back to some men who greeted us from the windows. I noticed that one of the cottages behind the guard post looked freshly painted and better kept than the rest. The porch was nice and neat, the windows sparkling clean and decorated with bright curtains. Then I glimpsed a young woman behind a slightly raised curtain at one window. She didn't look to me like a German auxiliary. Her face was serious, alert, and quite pretty, with a touch of make-up. She had smooth, black hair, meticulously groomed, with a blue ribbon. She turned around as if to speak to someone in the room, and a moment later I saw another head, this one blond and very young, right behind her. They looked at us, shook their heads in pity, and then the curtain was lowered and they were gone.

"*Puffkommando!* Did you see those two whores at the window?" asked the woman next to me.

No wonder the cottage was so well appointed, the girls so pretty and carefully made up. I thought at once of Lotti: she must be there too.

By now the whole Kommando had finished. The Kapo lined us up and we filed along to the exit, where once again the soldiers counted and inspected us, and we set off for Birkenau. We had taken only a few steps, though, when the air-raid siren went off: three long blasts and three short, meaning immediate danger and orders to take cover.

Chaos broke out, what with the men rushing back inside, the dogs barking, the *Posten* yelling "*los! los!*" Our Kapo wasn't sure what to do, but a soldier from the guard corps called us back in. Some women were pushed over toward a barrack, while I, along with several others, got shoved onto the porch of the curtained cottage. As the door was slammed shut we found ourselves in a dimly lit corridor with a flight of stairs in the center. It was very quiet, and instinctively we lowered our voices, the way you do in church.

One woman sat down to rest on the bottom stair, and another followed. A moment later the whole drab, shivering bunch of us were huddled on the stairs, straining our ears, aching to hear the grave, rhythmic rumble of the American fighter-bombers, the sweetest music on earth.

A slight noise startled us. The young brunette I had seen at the window was coming down the stairs, wearing a blue dress that matched her hair ribbon. She had a pleasant manner, and asked with a smile, "Are there any Romanians here?"

There weren't, but she invited us in all the same. She

had to keep urging until one woman finally took her up on it, and the rest of us trailed along up the spotless stairs, trying not to make too much noise with our clogs.

The Romanian led us down a hall with several doors opening off it, till we reached a room handsomely furnished with arm-chairs, sofas, mirrors, and a large glowing stove. We paused at the threshold, not daring to enter, and stared at the two women inside, one seated at a table in the center, apparently absorbed in the card game spread out before her, the other leaning against her chair, peering down as if eagerly awaiting the next move. They in turn looked us up and down in astonishment. The seated one was strikingly beautiful and dressed in a flashy, somewhat careless way — obviously a gypsy. The other one was fair, with strong features and a wary, stubborn expression; not even the gleaming golden hair framing her face could soften her looks.

"We have guests, Regine," our guide called out gaily. "Come in, why are you all standing at the door? It's not a *blockowa*'s room, you know. You won't be beaten if you cross the sacred threshold!"

We entered timidly, and even though it wasn't very cold, we were so drawn by the fire that we went straight for the stove, holding our chapped hands out over the majolica tiles.

The gypsy went back to shuffling her cards in silence, but the blond one came over and started asking a million questions — where were we from, how long had we been in the camp? She wanted to know if Maria la Morte was still the Kapo of lager B, and when she heard that she was, her eyes darkened.

"Ah, but it'll all be over," she muttered to herself, "it'll be over and she'll get what's coming to her."

Meanwhile the Romanian had brought out two huge rolls smelling of bacon and caraway seeds, with some pieces of smoked lard. She held them out to us. Our first reaction was utter disbelief. The next minute, one bold woman reached out her hand and everyone else immediately followed. And then our murmurs of ecstasy were smothered by the first mouthfuls.

Food! Each separate taste bud tingled with rapture, in a frenzy of pleasure at those fantastic, forgotten sensations. Our bodies shuddered with delight. We ate not just with our mouths, but with our noses, our eyes, our hands. Every sense we possessed was stimulated, taut, aroused by this incredible act.

We must have looked grotesque, for the blond woman broke out in great peals of laughter. Tossing back her splendid head, she laughed till the tears rolled down her cheeks. Even the gypsy laughed. Then the blond ran out and returned carrying a large pot full of split pea soup with potatoes.

"Go on, gobble up all you want, here's your chance!" She sounded like the sort who's entertained by the sight of starving dogs falling on food. We were humiliated, but nevertheless we tugged our spoons out of our waistbands and plunged them avidly into the pot.

Though I was totally caught up in the sensual pleasure of eating, at the back of my mind I still remembered Gustine's sister. She must be in the house. I wanted to see her. I had in fact been hoping that the door might open and Lotti appear, but since there was no such luck, I decided to ask the Romanian.

Lotti, the Dutch girl? Sure she was there, probably in her

room right now. She went to the door and called two or three times.

"What is it? Can't a person have a minute's peace?" came an irritated voice from down the hall.

"You have a visitor," called the Romanian. "A friend of yours from Birkenau wants to see you."

"A friend from Birkenau?" Now the voice was incredulous. "I'll be right there."

I waited in the doorway. In a minute or so, a door at the end of the hall flew open and there was Lotti, hastily pulling on a dressing gown. She came up to me and stared. When at last she recognized me, her eyes filled with tears. "Oh, Liana, Liana," she murmured, and led me down the hall to her room.

She looked so fresh and radiant that I was speechless. When she hugged and kissed me, she smelled wonderful, clean and sweet, with a tinge of face powder. I felt awkward and embarrassed, yet that didn't stop me from admiring the pink silk dressing gown clinging to her soft, rounded body.

"Come in, dear Liana," Lotti repeated.

The small room contained very little furniture besides the large unmade bed. Facing the bed hung a wide mirror. Even though it was late morning, the shutters were closed, and a small lamp on the nighttable cast a faint rosy glow rather than actual light.

"Come, Liana." Lotti made me sit on the bed and sat down beside me, clasping my hands. I looked in the mirror and did a double take. Could that face belong to me? It must, though I neither recognized nor liked it. Still, I couldn't resist studying it. It was impossible to accept that

that image was what I had become, that the face in the mirror was what people in the lager recognized as me.

"Listen, Liana," said Lotti, in a tone of resolve that hinted at inner turbulence. "Do you ever see my sister? I heard she's sick. Is she really very bad?"

I said yes, I had seen her, and though at first I'd planned not to mention the cigarette incident, I ended up telling her the whole story, omitting, of course, that Gustine had thrown away the package and told me Lotti was dead. Lotti heard me out with her head bowed. Either she could sense what I had left out, or else there had been similar episodes, for when I was done she looked up, her face grim with pain. "Gustine told you I was dead, didn't she?" she said. "She threw away the note and the cigarettes and said she didn't want anything to do with me, right?"

My confusion was answer enough. It was as if the dam holding back her tumultuous feelings collapsed, and all her pent-up grief, resentment, and despair came flooding out in great waves.

"She told you I was dead because I joined the *Puffkommando*, and she wouldn't touch the cigarettes because of how I got them. She thinks any decent girl would be tainted just handling them. Well, that's just not how it is. She's not fair. The only reason she didn't say bad things about me is because you're supposed to respect the memory of the dead."

I was very upset by her vehemence, indeed by the agony of her situation. I tried to break in, but Lotti brushed me aside and carried on, the words pouring out compulsively.

"But we really loved each other! How can two people be so close and live totally for each other, and then suddenly be farther apart than strangers or even enemies? Do you remember I told you how we were captured together in a police raid, and we didn't even get to see anyone again? We were crammed into that truck full of people frightened out of their wits, everyone was hysterical, completely falling apart. We were all we had left in the entire world. We didn't let each other out of our sight for the whole trip, and then for the entire time we spent in quarantine—we were so terrified of being separated.

"And then, you remember, we were both sent to work in that ghastly sewer Kommando—knee deep in water and slime all day long. We had to dig ditches near the crematoria where they could throw away the ashes, and it wasn't only the hard work, it was having to smell that smoke all the time. Just to see it—it was so thick and black, it looked like it would never dissolve and go away. Each time you picked your head up from the shovel and saw it hanging there you'd think, 'Another week, another month, then my turn.' I could actually feel it. I felt myself going up the chimney and over the roofs of the lager and vanishing little by little till there was no trace. No one would know I'd ever been alive.

"I used to remember a sermon our minister once gave. He was commenting on the Bible. It must have been the book of Job, yes, the part where Job just can't go on anymore and cries out in protest. He says, 'As the cloud is consumed and vanisheth away; so he that goeth down to the grave shall come up no more. He shall return no more to his house.' Well, I refused to be consumed and vanish like a cloud. I wanted to return to my house. I'm eighteen years old—I don't want to die. I know, no one wants to die, you'll tell me. But maybe I don't want to more than the others. Maybe that's the difference. Because I can feel how disgustingly wrong it is that I should have to die because I couldn't steal soup or I had no cigarettes to trade for bread, while other people who weren't as good as me, who might have committed crimes or led wicked lives, would somehow manage to survive. Oh sure, they'd still be here enjoying life, loving, singing, back home with their families. And where would I be? What would become of me? Just a black ribbon pinned to my family's clothes, a few pathetic words: 'Poor Lotti! What a pity she died so young!' And meanwhile, the streets are all lit up, people are singing new songs, there are flowers everywhere—but I'm not there to enjoy it because I died at Birkenau. Well, why do I have to accept all that? Who says I have to simply give up my life, just like that? Everyone in the lager goes around picking up leftovers from the garbage. They suck bones other people spit out—and I'm supposed to refuse life because it's offered on a dirty plate? I told Gustine all this, but she didn't understand. She suffered, sure, like everyone else, one torture after another, day after day, but she had no sense of the overall tragedy of it. She didn't know what I was talking about, and she got mad when I talked about death. She was always hoping for a miracle, always waiting for the war to end in two weeks. She'll be waiting till her last breath, and when she closes her eyes, she'll suffer less than I did in the sewers, believe me, because she won't think she's dying. Or even if she realizes it, she'll think it's God's will.

"She was always dragging God's name into it, Gustine was. It became an obsession with her. 'God won't forsake his creatures. God knows what he's doing. God can't allow injustice to triumph.' And meanwhile the crematorium just keeps puffing away and ashes are dropping on my head.

" 'That's your God over there!' I told her. She turned away and didn't answer. She had come to hate me, I could tell.

"Once we had the most evil Kapo, you know, one of the ones with the black triangle on their shirts—fat and sturdy and probably better dressed than she ever dreamed of at home. She managed to get whatever she wanted. I used to look at her and think, I'll go up in smoke and she'll still be around. She'll make it to the end of the war and go home happy and proud of herself. Is God aware of that, by any chance?

"What harm did I ever do, to be condemned like that? What did Gustine ever do? But it had reached a point where we could hardly talk to each other anymore. It felt like any words would destroy what was left of the bond between us. It was wearing down anyway, a little each day, like a candle. We still worked side by side, but without speaking, each of us locked in our own thoughts, sealed up in separate cocoons.

"People think blood ties mean everything. But what good is being brothers or sisters or whatever, when you see things in such opposite ways? The differences create such a barrier that you have no more in common than total strangers passing on the street. Gustine and I are of the same blood, we grew up together, but now there's nothing left between us, because I was afraid to die and she believed God would save her.

"I remember, the day before they asked for volunteers for the *Puff*, we had a quarrel and from then on we didn't speak a word. We slept together, and I heard her coughing all night long. I felt so sorry for her, I was almost in tears, but I just couldn't bring myself to say anything. She knew what

I was feeling too, but she just lay there and didn't make any move to get close again.

"It so happened that the very next morning the *blockowa* announced that anyone who wanted to go to the Auschwitz *Puffkommando* should report to her before roll-call. So I made up my mind. I waited till Gustine was off somewhere and went to the *blockowa*'s room. She was that tiny dark-haired one who screamed constantly, remember her? She knew right away why I was there. She said, 'Aha! So you want to go to the *Puff*? You want to have some fun and stuff your face, eh? How old are you?' 'Seventeen,' I said. She looked me over from head to foot and said I was a little thin. 'Please don't tell anyone I came,' I begged her, and she promised and sent me away. Two days later, just as I was about to march off with the Kommando, she called me out of line and had me stand apart. 'Why isn't my sister going to work?' Gustine asked. 'Because she's going to become a whore,' the *blockowa* answered, and everyone turned around to stare at me.

"Gustine came over, pale as a ghost. Her hands trembled. 'Is it true?' 'Yes,' I nodded. And she stepped back and said, 'Charlotte, from now on you're dead, you're not . . .'"

Lotti's voice had gotten shakier all along, and now she was so choked up she couldn't go on. Her words hung in the air as she fell back on the bed convulsively, burying her face in the pillow and sobbing desperately.

I tried to calm her, but it was no use. Her sobs only became more intense, and every few minutes she would cry out her sister's name. All I could do was stroke her soft blond hair and murmur soothing words. She must try to calm down, I said. I couldn't bear seeing her in such a state. Did she want me to leave feeling so awful?

I was going on this way when suddenly the half-open door was flung wide. In the doorway stood a soldier, a middle-aged *Posten* with a coarse, menacing face. First he asked what I was doing there, then he turned to Lotti, still weeping.

"What's the matter? What's going on here? What's all this whining? And why's everything closed up?"

He went to the window and flung open the shutters. Bright sunlight invaded the room.

"What are you whimpering about?" he asked Lotti again.

"Her sister is very sick," I answered.

"Her sister is sick? *Scheiss egal!* Who gives a shit?" the soldier thundered, unbuckling his belt. "*Scheiss egal!* Always the same old shit!"—that atrocious, despairing lager phrase they would repeat day in and day out, as if to confer on Cambronne's words the dignity of a philosophy.* "And you, beat it!"

The all clear was sounding, so I raced out without even saying good-bye to Lotti and joined the other women hurrying down the stairs. Outside, the whistles were calling the Kommandos to order. I took my place in line and gazed up at the sky. A wisp of smoke drifted overhead, carried on the wind from Birkenau to Auschwitz. Before too long, Gustine herself might be drifting slowly over that very house where Lotti lay weeping on the ample, unmade bed.

It was all nothing but smoke. Smoke drifting over the lagers, the town, and the brothel; smoke drifting over evil and innocence, wisdom and folly, death and life. All of it *"Scheiss egal."*

---

*Cambronne was a high-ranking French general who served under Napoleon and earned immortality of a sort by his famous response at the battle of Waterloo—"Merde," now known to every French schoolchild as "le mot Cambronne."—Tr. note

Hard Labor

"Look!" Lise whispered excitedly, tugging at my arm. "Look where Rosa's going!"

I was stretched out flat on my back on the verge of sleep, my apron over my face to shield it from the sun. These were the dog-days of summer: it was so scorchingly hot out in the field that I lay in a dizzy stupor. I sat up and reluctantly opened my eyes.

"What is it?" I grunted.

"Rosa just went over to the men's barrack. Erna too."

"So let them go. What do I care?"

I shrugged my shoulders. The earth's hot breath rose to envelop me as I lay back down, pulling my apron over my face. The other women too lay dazed on the yellow stubble under the sizzling August sun, their limp bodies streaming with sweat. Only Clari and a few of the younger girls were sitting up, chattering and shooting stray glances over toward the men.

We had been here for several days, since Mia, our Kapo, wouldn't willingly forfeit any place where she could rendez-vous with her *kochany*; through some deal worked out with the *Arbeitführer* she'd gotten herself assigned the task of clearing away the huge pile of rocks alongside the lager C warehouses and transporting them systematically up to the road.

Besides being pointless, this was excruciatingly dull work, made even more burdensome by the steady stream of soldiers and vehicles along the road. Moreover, since Mia was eager to impress the *Arbeitführer*, she insisted that we lug only the heaviest rocks. We were already nostalgic for the sand pits we used to curse so fervently. At least there we could stretch out in the shade during our break, while at this new site the soup was dished out right in the middle of the field, and only with the utmost caution did we dare edge our way into the patch of shadow cast by the building under construction. Inside, the Kapo passed the time undisturbed, eating the delicacies her *kochany* bestowed on her.

There were also several shacks used as toolsheds, where a men's Kommando spent the days quite comfortably. They were strapping young fellows with the breezy, impudent air of "well-organized" types, and whenever Mia retired to her suite, so to speak, they would take the opportunity to come out and parade in front of Rosa's and Erna's little circle, winking and pointing to the thick hunks of bread sticking up out of their pockets.

The women would banter a bit, laughing among themselves and acting coy, like women everywhere, until after a while they would slip away along the wall and into the sheds, to emerge only at the evening gong, all red and disheveled.

Rosa and Erna, the two young women from Warsaw whom the Kapo had taken under her wing, would come away with bowls heaped with Polish-style mashed potatoes, dripping with margarine and smelling of onions, and since they slept right below Lise and me, each night we witnessed them feasting with gusto. I generally looked the other way to spare myself this dubious pleasure, but Lise leaned out as far as she could go, as if she were trying to fall into the bowl, and kept careful track of how many mouthfuls Rosa and Erna each ate. Her greed was so unabashed that I often felt a kind of shame on her behalf and tried to pull her back on some pretext. But she wouldn't listen: with her face glued between her palms, she stared implacably at the spectacle, relenting only when the two blond girls started wiping their spoons.

"They've got the right idea. They're doing just fine," she would burst out, looking grim. "They certainly won't be breathing their last here. They're not stupid, that pair."

I had to agree that they weren't stupid, especially Erna, who had wangled her way into the Kapo's good graces and would surely go far.

But what did this have to do with me? It felt more natural for me to drift along with the current without making the slightest effort to reach the shore, and so Lise's morbid interest in our neighbors' fortunes felt totally irrelevant. The next time she tugged at my arm I didn't bother to hide my annoyance.

"What do you want now?" I grumbled. "Leave me alone."

Lise informed me that the old warehouse Kapo was fooling around with Erna too, and she had already gotten two delicious bowls of soup out of him. With carrots, no less!

"Well, what do I care? Go ahead and do it, make up your mind once and for all," I snapped. "Why destroy yourself with envy when you can easily have what you want? Go right ahead."

Oh, it was all very well to talk, Lise snapped back, but she'd left a husband behind. She wasn't like those little tarts who for a slice of bread would spread themselves out for half the camp. She was a respectable woman who loved her husband.

"In that case, shut up about it."

No, she couldn't! How could a person shut up in the face of such injustice? The ones who turned professional would go home triumphant, covered with glory, while the honorable ones would sooner or later end up in the crematorium. For her part she wouldn't even care that much, but she had to get back for Rudi's sake. She loved her Rudi too much to lose him without a struggle.

At that point I could only sigh with resignation, for once Lise got going on the subject of Rudi, there was no escape. She had spoken at such length about her young husband, I knew his habits, tastes, and failings so thoroughly and could discuss him myself with such authority, that anyone would think I was married to him too. But apparently I still didn't know him well enough, since Lise always managed to dig up some hitherto unrevealed detail.

She was just launching into her speech when the lager C gong sounded and Mia appeared in the doorway, straightening her white silk scarf and calling for us to line up. One by one the women rose slowly to their feet, wiping their red faces, and got in line as the men seated snugly against the barrack wall looked on.

"My feet are all swollen," Lise whined when we got to the road. "These clogs are so heavy, I can't take another step. You're so lucky, you can go barefoot."

I had tossed my clogs over my shoulder and was stepping gingerly on the hot grayish dirt road. Meanwhile, Lise made the same complaint every day but would never venture going barefoot: It was too painful, she said; she wasn't used to it. Well, did she think I was?

I stole a bitter glance at her graceful petite figure and her round red querulous face. Suddenly I was seething with malice. I was willing to bet she'd burst into tears any minute now. With mounting rage, I deliberately shuffled my feet to stir up the dust. Let her have something to complain about! I could understand, now, why the Ukrainians in the field squads would beat up the frail women who couldn't manage to hoist the enormous sheaves or line them up nimbly. There is truly nothing so insufferable as futile complaints and the inability to adapt.

Once at the work site I left off fretting over Lise and started hunting for just the right kind of rocks. The first few days we would pick them up at random, but it didn't take long to discover that certain flat and seemingly bulky ones were actually very light, while some of the smaller ones were so heavy that your back ached lugging them around. Thus we'd all grown highly selective, climbing up the huge pile to choose our stones and rolling them down to the bottom.

"Leave those alone!" I yelled. It was old Adela, looking sneaky. "Those are mine, I rolled them down there! Thief!"

But Adela nonchalantly appropriated the rocks and sauntered off without a word, leaving me to follow along, muttering to myself as I dragged a few small stones. Then I began all over again, the same as the other women scattered here and there throughout the stony, dug-up field. Moving as slowly as we could, each of us would pick out a stone, carry it wearily to the edge of the road, and turn back to repeat the process. We kept up the identical motions all morning, all afternoon, until the evening gong, when Mia called us to line up for the return trip.

I usually worked next to Lise, chatting about this and that or asking her to sing, for she had a lovely voice and knew lots of songs. And that was not all her talent: when she managed to lay hands on a scrap of glossy paper, she'd fold it over the broken comb that was the sum of her worldly possessions, and blow on it. Her excellent renditions of *"La paloma"* and *"J'attendrai"* had won her an admiring entourage: not a Sunday passed without some woman dropping by our bunk to hear Lise play on the comb.

"A week before I was arrested, my husband gave me this beautiful accordion," Lise never failed to tell us. "That was his last gift. I wonder where it is now?"

To console her, we'd say, "He'll give you an even better one."

But Lise shook her head. Her hazel eyes, flecked with the green and rust shades of autumn, were ruefully skeptical. How would she ever have an accordion again? She couldn't even get a decent bit of soup! She couldn't even . . .

With my right hand holding the rock in place on my shoulder, I passed the time murmuring beloved lines of poetry and long passages from the classics I had studied in school. My favorites were Homer and Catullus, but there was also a certain canto from the *Inferno* about the damned who carry rocks. . . . I tried my best to remember it, berating myself for having been such a lazy student.

Back and forth I trudged, automatically lining up the rocks, drifting in another world. Several times I nearly walked right into the pile, as the other women looked askance and Mia shouted: Was I drunk, by any chance, or what?

Soon Lise was back. "Guess what Erna told me," she said. "There's this foreman who has a really great harmonica and she told him I could play, so he's coming to hear me tomorrow. It could be my lucky day! Do you think he might give me something?"

I yielded to curiosity. "Which one is he?"

"That tall young one. His name is Sergio, Erna said. He passed by just before, while you were asleep, and looked at me."

So we got to talking as usual, and bit by bit my anger subsided. After all, Lise was one of the few people in the Kommando I enjoyed talking to; at least she had decent manners. She must find me somewhat withdrawn, and I could hardly blame her for taking advantage of my silence to indulge her own feelings.

The sun wheeled slowly across the bright blue sky. Scanning its position, I tried to guess the time. I had become very adept at this antique skill and took great pride in it: often the women would come to consult me.

"It's almost time for the gong," I declared.

When the three long peals sounded a few minutes later, the women shrieked with joy, throwing down their stones and racing to get in line. Mia counted us, and we started toward the road, as a calm summer sunset hovered over the faded countryside.

In the row ahead, Rosa and Erna laughed and prattled as always, tossing their heads so the soft blond highlights glinted in the sun. Summer had tinged their skin golden, and if not for a hard, ambiguous shrewdness playing over their features, they might easily have been taken for two young girls on their way home from the beach.

"Hey, Lise!" The blue-eyed Erna turned and gave a cunning wink. "Music tomorrow, right?"

"Yes, yes," replied Lise. Then she quickly tried to appear casual about it, for beside her, Elenka and Nina, the sour "crematorium sisters," shot evil looks from their piercing eyes.

"Aha, you too?" said Nina. "So you're falling for it too."

But Rosa and Erna, who detested the dreary old maids and had dubbed them "crematorium sisters" because of their invariably glum tone, spared Lise any further discomfort. Whatever it was they hissed in Polish was so effective that the two sisters backed down, grumbling, and finally gave up altogether.

At last we reached the lager, and once the evening rituals were done, I stretched out contentedly on my mat.

"Where were you?" I asked Lise when she returned carrying a bucket of water. "Where'd you get that?"

"I took it from the *stubowa*. I'm going to rinse out my dress," Lise explained, starting to peel it off. "Do you want to wash?"

I hesitated, feeling too lazy, but when I saw the circle of applicants forming around her, I roused myself.

"All right, as soon as you're done. I'm not washing my dress, though. I don't want to put it back on dripping wet."

Sluggishly, I turned over on my side: I had finished my bread, and now was the moment I thought of as "curtain time." In the dusky half-light, the women wandered about laughing, crying, singing, as I observed dispassionately from on high.

Lise stood naked with one leg in the bucket, energetically rubbing her slender white body. She doesn't even need a bra, I noted: her pointy breasts rose to two delicate pink tips.

She asked if I'd scrub her back. She had a sliver of soap left over from last month, but it was too encrusted with sand to be of any use, so I tossed it in the bucket and began on her dress. The water petitioners were waiting patiently when all of a sudden a big brawny *stubowa* came thundering down the hall looking for her stolen bucket: she needed it to give out the coffee. What kind of filthy tricks were we up to now?

"*Oh, Schweine,*" she yelled raucously and yanked at the bucket, while Lise tried to hang on so the water and the dress wouldn't get dumped on the floor. In the end the *stubowa* got it away and trounced off to fill it with coffee. Lise lay down alongside me, all wet and cool.

"Who are you getting so prettied up for?" I teased. "The foreman with the harmonica?"

To my great surprise, she turned somber and her eyes filled with tears.

"I'm sorry," I said contritely. "I didn't mean to hurt your feelings."

She shook her head as if to say it wasn't my fault, then turned her back, pretending to sleep. Meanwhile the other women complained about the wet dress hanging from the beams: they bumped into it whenever they moved, and it was dripping on them, besides.

"Good night, Lise," I said softly. But I got no reply, so I closed my eyes to escape from my troubles too.

In the morning, Lise took up her theme again. She had dreamed of Rudi, she told me. He was watching for her from the window of their house, looking worried and upset. She came running and waited for him to open the door, but instead he disappeared without a word, leaving her desolate out on the street, panting for breath.

"I woke up crying." She paused, musing, on a pile of rocks. "I can still see him looking so worn out and wretched. . . . What do you suppose it means?"

The meaning struck me as abundantly clear: Lise's husband would not appreciate his wife's efforts to supplement her diet. She'd return home to find bitterness and rejection. But since I didn't want to assume the responsibility, I offered a diplomatic response.

"It means he's thinking of you," I asserted. "It's only natural that he feels unhappy. How else could he feel, with no news of you for so long?"

So Lise persuaded herself that that must be the case: Rudi must be sick with heartache, not knowing where or how she was. Oh, if he could just picture the state she was in! Rudi, who could call two doctors for a common cold!

"To tell the truth, you don't look bad at all," I said. She looked trim and neatly decked out in the clean blue dress. "This morning you look really pretty. Even your lips have some color."

Lise smiled happily, running off to borrow Erna's fragment of mirror to study herself at length. After the gong, sitting in the shadow of the half-built house, she kept smoothing down her short black hair.

The soup was burning hot, so I set my bowl on the ground and waited for it to cool. Rosa and Erna ambled by and paused in front of us.

"Hey, Lise," Erna said impatiently. "Are you coming?"

With her spoon poised in mid-air, Lise looked up, blushing. Feeling embarrassed for her, I bent over as if to stir my soup.

"So?" Erna repeated. "Coming?"

"I'll just finish my soup. It's very hot," Lise stammered, and she made a show of blowing on it. Rosa and Erna strolled on. Even though I was looking the other way, Lise's struggle was so palpable that I would surely have said something, but at that instant a male voice boomed out right

behind us. We spun around. A young man wearing a foreman's red armband and holding a harmonica stood gazing
smugly down at Lise. He was quite tall, and despite his
shaved head, which didn't improve his appearance, he had
a broad winning smile and dazzling white teeth. He leaned
down and winked.

"Hey you, little lady," he said. "Can you play?"

Lise smiled up at him and reached for the harmonica.
But Sergio was clearly a self-confident type and hardly
inclined to hand over his possessions so readily. He laughed
and pulled it back.

"Aha," he said coolly. "So you like it?"

Just then Erna appeared out of nowhere and snatched it
away with a mischievous show of force. So Lise got to play,
and we gathered round to listen and admire. She had barely
finished when we chorused, "Encore, encore!"

This time Lise went all out, lavishing the best of her
repertoire—*"Bel ami,"* "Silver Star," *"La paloma"*—while
the imposing Sergio knelt close by her, listening with uncon-
cealed pleasure.

"Brava!" he said, and reached out to take her arm, man-
aging to brush against her breast.

"You, little lady, no *kochany?*"

"No *kochany!*" replied Lise, drawing back.

"But how come? And so pretty, too."

He moved even closer, putting his arm around her waist
as he spoke, his lips grazing her neck and ear. A few people
noticed and ogled in silence, until Lise finally stood up,
somewhat pale.

"No *kochany*," she said firmly. "A husband."

"Husband? Where, husband? In lager?"

Lise shook her head, no, pantomiming that he was far away. Sergio chortled and pointed a finger at the camp D smokestack, sending up grayish black billows.

"Husband? Husband *scheiss!* Crematorium, then no more husband!"

Suddenly Mia appeared and, seeing Sergio among us, started screaming. He walked airily away, whistling a tune, as Mia came over and smacked Lise, then kicked over our bowls, which in my case was most unfortunate as it was still full.

"I can't! I just can't do it!" wailed Lise that evening as we lay on our mats. It was the hour for whispering secrets. "I've never done anything like that. I can't demean myself like those women who sell themselves for a piece of bread, or like the Kapo—I mean, they were probably in business before. How could I go back to Rudi after such awful things? He'd be so glad to have me back, the poor guy, he'd never know. But I'd know! How could I ever look him in the eye again? How could I live with myself, with my conscience? I'm sure God would punish me for deceiving him, wouldn't he?"

"Uh . . ." I said.

"Will you stop saying Uh, uh, like a cow! Help me get things in the proper perspective. What's the right thing to do? I can either betray my husband and stay alive for him, or be faithful and desert him—because I'm sure to die here in Birkenau."

I tried hard to give this dilemma some serious thought, but got nowhere. There was the image of an impeccably chaste Lise ascending to heaven with the palm and halo of martyrdom, but the underside showed her husband devastated and alone in a shattered home. On the other hand, Lise could return bright and smiling to Rudi's embrace after the war, and yet in her smile might just lurk something unctuous and professional—owing, possibly, to an excess of margarine procured for her lager bread.

"When we were married," Lise went on, "I swore to be faithful in the eyes of the law."

"Well, but how could the law foresee that you'd end up in Birkenau?"

"So you're saying yes?"

"I'm not saying anything. Is your husband the jealous type?"

"What on earth does jealousy have to do with it? You never understand a thing. Do you honestly think I'd consider doing this because I like Sergio? I don't give a damn about Sergio. If I deceive my husband, it's because I love him, because I want to see him again and make him happy and spend the rest of my life with him. Not for fun, for God's sake! It's not some casual whim. I'm not the type to take this sort of thing lightly. If anything I've been too scrupulous that way. And you'd call this being unfaithful?"

"Then go ahead and sacrifice yourself. What do you want me to say? Make up your own mind!"

"Make up my mind! That's easy enough to say. But when you love someone as much as I love Rudi! Besides, the war could be over any minute. I've made it this far, why should I ruin myself at the last minute? Oh, God, God! We've been suffering so long, why doesn't God do something for us? And yet . . . it would really take so little to escape from all this. Did you know Mina's been transferred? She's in the dressmaking squad. She's got all the comforts of home."

I laughingly suggested that Lise follow Mina's example. Why not seduce the formidable *Frau* Gotti, Kapo of the dressmakers and renowned for her lesbian predilections? When Mina still slept in our barrack, we used to hear *Frau* Gotti's heavy, resounding footsteps every morning as she came to wake her lover with a long kiss as well as a little snack.

"*Frau* Gotti? No, no!" She was horror-struck.

"Well, why not? Is Sergio any better?"

Lise was outraged. There was no point even talking to me, she declared, and appealed next to Lillike, a superstitious Hungarian blabbermouth who regularly spent half her weekly ration of margarine on having her fortune told by Madame Louise. After paying close attention to the ins and outs of Lise's predicament, Lillike was of the opinion that not even Madame Louise's cards could be trusted in so weighty a case. What Lise needed was an immediate consultation with Maria of the Miracle, the saint who talked to the spirits. She alone was in a position to pass judgment.

"Maria of the Miracle!" I was flabbergasted. "Who's she?"

Lillike couldn't get over my ignorance. Had I never seen the woman dressed in rags who pulled the lager A *Scheisskommando* (Shit Kommando) cart, shouting prayers at the top of her lungs? Why, the entire camp knew Maria of the Miracle.

"Oh, yes, I remember," I said. "Wasn't there some involved story about her? Why is she called Maria of the Miracle?"

Lillike proceeded to tell how this poor lady, Marie, was arrested in Vienna and deported because she'd hidden away a bit of sugar for her sick husband. As might be expected, she was soon in the infirmary and one unlucky day was picked in a selection and put in the rest Block for several weeks. Then one night the truck came for the whole bunch of them. They were herded on, more dead than alive, and deposited at the door of Crematorium Number 2, right outside the camp—a house with a handsome red tower and blossoming flower-beds around the entrance. The windows were barred, however, and from within flickered a sickly yellow, spectral light.

When they found themselves at the door, the women broke out in the usual howls and shrieks and absolutely refused to enter. These screams would be loud enough to be heard in the barracks, where the women who had to get up for work the next day lay sleepless and distraught.

By kicking and beating them with sticks, the guards finally managed to get them into the huge room. Except for one, clinging to the arm of a soldier who was about to shut the door on the thrashing, doomed crowd: *Frau* Marie, with her glittery eyes.

"Inside!" he ordered—a rosy-cheeked boy with clear pale blue eyes. He tried to get away, to shove her off, but she grabbed him by the wrists and stared as if she were possessed.

"I am your mother!" said the crazed old woman, and the boy recognized the crisp Viennese accent.

"I am your mother! How can you kill me? You wouldn't kill your own mother!"

She squeezed his wrists tighter, breathing her mad words into his face. The boy was uneasy, especially as the door wasn't completely closed and the others strained against it with all their might. It was his first time at this assignment; he didn't want any trouble. So the best he could do was close the door, leaving Maria outside. When he realized his error, he shrugged his shoulders and assumed a decisive air.

"Your turn will come, you goddamned witch," he threatened. "You're just an old witch! You hexed me!"

And thus Marie returned to the camp to become Maria of the Miracle, for indeed what miracle could be greater than this one performed through her?—moving the heart of a young SS man to a good deed.

Day and night Maria prayed to the Savior, conversed with the spirits, and gave wise counsel: Maria of the Miracle, a regular saint.

"Oh, come on," I protested, appalled. "You actually believe this story? She's probably some lunatic who invented it to get attention."

But of course Lise and Lillike stood their ground, affirming that the story was gospel truth. Maria was a saint, and I understood nothing. Any discussion would be in vain, I could see, human credulity and bias being all the more tenacious when they seem to yield some advantage. I simply turned away to greet a French friend passing by.

"Good evening, Madame Odette. How are you?"

"Good evening, Mademoiselle Liane. Not bad, thanks. How have you been lately?"

Ah, the blessed French! They were the only people in the lager whose courtesy and breeding never deserted them. They could eat elegantly out of a bowl balanced on their knees; their conversation was punctuated by *"Madame"* and *"s'il vous plaît."* In the midst of the lager's bestial crudity they alone maintained a tone of refined, dignified civility; the same women who never neglected to dab their faces with leftover margarine would also intrepidly confront a *stubowa* who was roughing up some fellow prisoner.

And so I washed my hands of Lise's problems and their absurd remedies and wouldn't have addressed another word to her, had she not come up to me the following morning in a friendly way.

"Would you do something for me?" she asked. "I want to look for Maria at the Polish women's Mass and Lillike can't go. Would you come?"

It was Sunday morning, and I was just wondering if I might slip away at the critical moment of going to fetch the soup. It was partly curiosity and partly my urge to get away from the barrack: I agreed.

The camp had its usual Sunday look. It was a clear, bright morning, and the refreshing country air was a pleasure to breathe.

"Where is it?"

Lise pointed toward Barrack 27, way at the far end of the camp, where from time immemorial, sinks were being installed. Every morning, including Sundays, men would report to work there, mostly "organizers" and Kapos who used this pretext to pay a visit to their *kochani* in the lager. Once they arrived, they promptly shifted roles—from construction workers to Don Giovannis—transforming the future washroom into a subsidiary branch of the Auschwitz brothel.

Meanwhile the old women would assemble each Sunday behind the shelter of the walls, clutching primitive crucifixes cut out of cast-off boxes or rosaries acquired at who knows what sacrifices. Paying no heed to what went on in the doorway and inside the barrack frequented by the camp's beauties, they knelt on the ground to pray, while behind the brick partition the others lay with their *kochani* on sacks of cement—each group, in its divergent way, seeking salvation.

Lise touched one of the kneeling women on the shoulder. "Where is Maria of the Miracle?" The old woman looked up, startled, and Lise repeated her question. Without interrupting her prayers, the woman jerked her head toward the sky.

"What?" gasped Lise, frightened. "Maria . . . ?"

The woman nodded upwards again, then bent her head between her palms, lost in fervent prayer, as Lise stood there foolishly.

"Come on, let's go," I called. "Don't you get it? Even your Maria of the Miracle is gone. That's the end of that."

But after only a few steps I paused—the women were beginning the litanies.

"*Mater purissima!*" one chanted. The others responded in unison.

"*Mater inviolata! Mater consacrata!*"

With eyes lowered, we listened to the familiar words, as the fragrance of incense and roses seemed to rise up from the stony road. In the dimming light gleamed the altar's precious stones. We could feel the cool holy water on our fingers.

"*Rosa mistica! Stella matutina!*"

As the organ notes resounded in our minds, our throats tightened; we yearned for succor, love, peace.

A brusque male voice shocked us back to Birkenau.

"Oho, the little lady! Saying your prayers?"

Sergio loomed up before us, a tall figure haloed by the sun, with narrow eyes twinkling in his swarthy face.

"What about you, don't you pray?" returned Lise.

"What, me? Oh, no. We all got to go sooner or later, pray or no pray."

He stood motionless, eyes greedily devouring Lise, desire radiating so powerfully from him that I felt like an intruder and started to move off.

"No, wait, I'm going with you," Lise cried.

He gripped her by the wrist, staring into her eyes until she abruptly broke away.

"My friend has to get back," she told him. "Good-bye."

She took my arm and we left. But at the barrack door she stopped, saying she'd lost her handkerchief.

"I'll go see if I can find it. I just got it yesterday and I'd hate to lose it."

So I went in by myself. When Lillike asked for Lise, I said she'd gone to look for her handkerchief and would be right back.

Lise returned quite late though, having found not only the handkerchief but some bread and a harmonica as well.

❀

Jewish Lives

THOMAS TOIVI BLATT
From the Ashes of Sobibor: A Story of Survival

IDA FINK
A Scrap of Time

LALA FISHMAN AND STEVEN WEINGARTNER
Lala's Story: A Memoir of the Holocaust

LISA FITTKO
Solidarity and Treason: Resistance and Exile, 1933–1940

PETER FURST
Don Quixote in Exile

SALOMEA GENIN
Shayndl and Salomea: From Lemberg to Berlin

RICHARD GLAZAR
Trap with a Green Fence: Survival in Treblinka

ROBERT B. GOLDMANN
Wayward Threads

HENRYK GRYNBERG
Children of Zion

ERICH LEYENS AND LOTTE ANDOR
Years of Estrangement